lyndey milan's
fabulous food

lyndey milan's
fabulous
food

photography by Michael Cook

NEW HOLLAND

For Michael Cook — for your sense of humour, passion for food, photographic talent and all that you have taught me — I enjoy you!

First published in Australia in 1999 by New Holland Publishers (Australia) Pty Ltd
Sydney • Auckland • London • Cape Town

Produced and published in Australia by New Holland Publishers (Australia) Pty Ltd
14 Aquatic Drive Frenchs Forest NSW 2086 Australia
1A/278 Lake Road Northcote Auckland New Zealand
24 Nutford Place London w1H 6DQ United Kingdom
80 McKenzie Street Cape Town 8001 South Africa

National Library of Australia
Cataloguing-in-Publication data:

Milan, Lyndey.
  Lyndey Milan's fabulous food
  Includes Index

  ISBN 1 86436 512 9
  1. Quick and easy cookery 2. Cookery. I. Title
  641.5

Publishing General Manager: Jane Hazell
Publisher: Averill Chase
Project Coordinator: Julie Nekich
Editor: Lynn Cole
Designer: Peta Nugent
Accessories: Accoutrement
Reproduction: Colour Symphony, Singapore
Printer: South China Printing Co. Ltd

contents

introduction

I have been thrilled with the response to my first books, **Plates** and **Flavours**. Producing a book is like having a baby — you take care during gestation to ensure a smooth and happy delivery into the world. Then, you proudly show off your offspring, delighted that complete strangers should find your progeny as appealing as you do.

However, your children, and your books, take on a life of their own. Your books as others interpret and adapt your recipes, your children as they establish their independence. But both have an unmistakable genetic and environmental heritage. So, these recipes truly reflect my life — some developed after inspiring trips to Morocco, Portugal, Asia and around Australia, others for cooking or food-and-wine-matching classes. Some began life in my 'Fast & Fabulous' column in **Australian Good Taste** magazine or 'Fast & Easy' column in **The Sydney Weekly**. Others are here just because I love them — all taste fabulous. Like you I have an incredibly busy life, but I am not willing to compromise on flavour in food. Besides, my children would never tolerate it! So I cook as simply as possible — either the whole dish is fast, or if it takes a little longer to cook, the preparation is minimal. Once again, Michael Cook's glorious photos look good enough to eat — there is no artifice here, just fresh, fabulous food cooked and presented immediately. Having a passion for the increased pleasure gained from successful food and wine matching, I have made suggestions here too.

Finally thanks to my family, especially Blair and Lucy, friends and supporters — and to my publisher, Averill Chase, for her persistence, good humour and patience.

Keep cooking and you'll keep smiling.

Food for those informal occasions, or just 'cause you feel like a kid and want to eat with your hands.

Finger Food

These delightful little finger food items can be made larger to serve as an entree. I use the delicious Persian fetta in olive oil, from Yarra Valley Dairy, but if you can't get this, use goat curd or ricotta.

INGREDIENTS

Makes 18 tarts

2 sheets butter puff pastry

4–6 vine-ripened tomatoes, thinly sliced

2 tablespoons tapenade (see recipe page 60)

345g (11oz) fetta cheese

fresh oregano

Preheat oven to hot, 220°–230°C (450°–475°F) Gas Mark 6. Line a flat baking tray with baking paper. Using a pastry cutter, cut pastry into 6–7 cm rounds (you should get 18 rounds). Place on baking paper and prick all over with a fork. Cover with another sheet of baking paper and another oven tray. (This prevents the puff pastry, chosen for its superior flavour, from rising.) Place in oven and cook for 10–15 minutes, or until golden brown. Remove from oven and cool. Just before serving, place a tomato slice on each pastry base, spread with tapenade, top with a small scoop of cheese and garnish with oregano.

Choose semillon for a sublime combination with tomato or, if you prefer a red wine, try chambourcin or pinot noir.

tomato tarts with fetta and tapenade

bessara

This is a Moroccan recipe, a little like Middle Eastern hummus. Traditionally it is made with fava beans or broad beans, but as these have to be soaked overnight and are not always easy to get, use any variety of canned white bean. The result is similar. Serve with pide or pitta bread, raw vegetables, or pitta crisps – made by cutting up pitta bread, sprinkling with lemon pepper (optional), and toasting in the oven.

Makes about 1^1/$_2$ cups

Chop garlic and parsley together in a blender or food processor. Add drained beans and remaining ingredients, except paprika and pitta bread, and blend to a smooth paste. If it is too thick, add 1 or 2 tablespoons of water.

Transfer to a serving bowl and sprinkle with a little paprika.

Choose a semillon as a good match for the quite dominant garlic in this dip or, if served as an appetiser, perhaps a chilled fino sherry.

INGREDIENTS

2 cloves garlic

^{1}/$_4$ bunch Continental parsley

300g (10oz) canned cooked white beans, e.g. fava, broad, cannelini, butter beans

1^1/$_2$ teaspoons cumin

^{1}/$_4$ cup (60ml/2fl oz) olive oil

^{1}/$_3$ teaspoon sweet paprika, to garnish

pitta bread, to serve

polenta canapes with prawns

I developed this recipe for an Epicurean Tour, involving a tasting at the store of Simon Johnson, Purveyor of Quality Foods, and finishing at the Sydney Fish Markets for a cooking class using some of the ingredients we had seen. All was then matched with wine. What a day!

INGREDIENTS

2 cups (500ml/16fl oz) water

$1/2$ cup (85g/3oz) polenta (cornmeal)

$1/4$ cup freshly grated parmesan cheese

2 teaspoons chopped fresh basil

2 tablespoons butter, cut into cubes

salt and freshly ground black pepper

20–30 cooked prawns (depending on size), shelled and deveined

2 tablespoons pesto

basil leaves, to garnish (optional)

Makes about 30 canapes

Bring salted water to the boil. Lower heat to medium and slowly add polenta, whisking as you go. Continue to whisk for up to 10 minutes as the mixture thickens. (You may find it easier to use a wooden spoon.) Continue to cook, stirring occasionally, until the mixture is very thick and comes away from the side of the pan. Add parmesan, basil and butter and season to taste with salt and pepper. Pour into a tray lined with baking paper and refrigerate until set. Using a small pastry cutter, cut into circles (or use a knife to cut into squares or diamonds for less wastage) and reheat in a moderate oven, 180°–190°C (350°–375°F) Gas Mark 4, for 5–10 minutes or on the grill (the grill gives the best texture if you have time). Cut prawns in half, if large, and place on polenta rounds. Top with a little pesto and garnish with basil leaves.

Choose a chilled sherry, good-quality sparkling wine or champagne to serve with canapes.

scallops on the shell
with Asian-style vinaigrette

This is a recipe I made up on the spur of the moment. It was 6.30pm and my dinner guests were due in an hour. I wanted something informal to serve with drinks in place of an entree. I had beautiful scallops and just raided my cupboard to come up with something to go with them.

Serves 6

With motor running, drop garlic and ginger into the food processor to chop. Add parsley and, when chopped, add mirin, salt and oil. Process until combined. Spoon over scallops and place under the grill for only a few moments, until scallops are opaque and just warm. Serve immediately.

Choose a full-fruited wine as this dressing is rather sweet – chardonnay, riesling or pinot noir would be perfect.

INGREDIENTS

1 clove garlic

2–3 slices fresh ginger

$1/2$ cup Continental parsley

2 tablespoons mirin

pinch of rock salt

$2/3$ cup (160ml/5fl oz) extra virgin olive oil

36 scallops, on the shell

chicken, preserved lemon and green olive kofta

INGREDIENTS

1/2 cup Continental parsley

1/2 cup coriander (cilantro)

1/4 preserved lemon (skin only)

4 thick slices stale white bread
(crusts removed)

60g (2oz) green olives, stoned and cracked

2 teaspoons cumin

pepper

chilli powder, to taste

410g (13oz) chicken mince

olive oil

chutney, to serve (optional)

sauce

2 cloves garlic, crushed

2 tablespoons mint,
finely chopped

3/4 cup (190ml/6fl oz) thick
Greek-style yoghurt,
approx.

While many of us avoid deep-frying for health reasons, this is one of the oldest and most popular cooking methods in the Mediterranean basin, where they prefer to use olive oil for the purpose. Always cook at around 180°C (350°F) for a crisp, dry finish. This recipe comes from my colleague Mary McMahon.

Makes about 20 balls

With food processor motor running continuously, add ingredients for chicken balls, except oil, in order listed and process until combined. With wet hands, roll 2-teaspoon portions of mixture into small balls. Ideally, refrigerate for 30 minutes.

Deep-fry, in batches, in olive oil for 4 minutes, or until golden. Drain on paper towels and serve with chutney and/or sauce made by mixing garlic, mint and yoghurt.

Choose an Italian wine or varietal of Italian origin, a grenache/shiraz/mourvedre blend, or a young semillon.

Simple and stylish, this idea can be used as finger food with cocktails or as an entree. Either way it is delicious and easy.

potato roesti with seared beef and wasabi

Makes 22

Combine marinade ingredients and marinate beef for several hours or overnight, turning occasionally.

Peel and grate potatoes; place in a bowl, and cover with cold water to prevent discoloration. Melt a little butter in a large pan, electric frypan or on a flatplate. Squeeze handfuls of potato dry and fry in small rounds – you can neaten the shapes by using a 5–6cm (2–2$\frac{1}{2}$in) round pastry cutter. Push down with the back of a spoon to compress. (Once each roesti has begun to set and cook, the pastry cutter can be removed and reused for the next roesti.) When golden brown turn over and fry other side until golden. Repeat with remaining butter and potato until all roestis are cooked. Alternatively, once lightly golden on both sides, they can be finished off in a hot oven for 5–10 minutes. These can be made well in advance of serving. Serve warm or at room temperature.

Pan-fry rump at high temperature for only about 2 minutes each side to keep medium rare. (Fillet can be sealed in a pan and cooked in a hot oven for 5–10 minutes.) Remove from heat and rest for 10 minutes before slicing.

To assemble, combine crème fraîche and wasabi and spread on roestis. Top with slices of beef. Garnish each with a tip of rocket leaf.

Surprisingly, wasabi is wonderful with sparkling wine and champagne. Choose a rosé style here, to further complement the beef.

INGREDIENTS

500g (1lb) thick piece of rump steak or eye fillet

4 medium to large potatoes, about 850g (1$\frac{3}{4}$lbs)

60g (2oz) butter

250g (8oz) crème fraîche

2 teaspoons wasabi

baby rocket leaves, to garnish

marinade

$\frac{1}{4}$ cup (60ml/2fl oz) kecap manis (Indonesian soy sauce) or soy sauce

1 tablespoon honey

1 clove garlic, crushed or 1 teaspoon crushed garlic

1 teaspoon grated ginger

1 teaspoon Chinese five spice

1 tablespoon sherry or sake

1 teaspoon sesame oil

lamb cutlets with mint pesto

INGREDIENTS

2–3 lamb cutlets per person

Thai sweet chilli sauce

mint pesto

75g (3½oz) parmesan cheese

3 cloves garlic

1 bunch fresh mint leaves

pinch of salt

90g (3oz) blanched almonds, roasted (see Note)

½ cup (125ml/4fl oz) olive oil

Any kind of pesto would be delicious with perfectly cooked, plump, pink lamb cutlets. However, mint and lamb are traditional partners and mint with a hint of chilli is doubly refreshing. The cutlets make ideal finger food.

Pesto serves 6–8

Brush cutlets with chilli sauce and place under preheated grill for 2–3 minutes each side (keep a close eye on them as the sugar in the chilli sauce burns easily).

For pesto, grate cheese in a food processor. Remove grating attachment and put in chopping blade. Add garlic and, when chopped, add mint and salt and process to a puree. Add almonds and process to combine. Slowly pour in oil, a little at a time, until pesto is smooth and well combined.

Note: Roast almonds in a moderate oven, 180°–190°C (350°–375°F) Gas Mark 4, for 5–10 minutes, or microwave on high on a layer of paper towels for 1 minute at a time until golden.

Choose a cabernet sauvignon, many of which have minty characters.

OK, so you don't feel like cooking tonight.
Dead simple dishes to entice you into
the kitchen…briefly.

I don't want
to cook

chillied garlic pasta

This is my version of an Italian classic. It's simple and delicious.

Serves 4

Cook pasta in plenty of boiling salted water, according to directions on packet. Stir once or twice to prevent sticking.

Meanwhile, heat 1 or 2 tablespoons olive oil in a pan and cook garlic, chilli and anchovies (the anchovy fillets will soon disintegrate). When the pasta is al dente (or still just firm to the teeth), drain it and immediately mix the anchovy mixture through, along with the parsley. Serve immediately with salt, pepper and olive oil to taste.

Choose a pinot noir, grenache or grenache/shiraz blend.

INGREDIENTS

500g (1lb) good quality pasta (e.g. bavette)

extra virgin olive oil

5 cloves garlic, sliced

3 red chillies, seeded and chopped

5 anchovy fillets

1/4 cup freshly chopped parsley

salt and freshly ground pepper

grilled caesar salad

Some time ago I visited the beautiful Margaret River area of Western Australia, a superb wine-growing region. The region is also noted for some terrific food. At Vasse Felix winery I was very impressed with this rather unusual version of the caesar salad.

Serves 2

Make the dressing by placing egg yolks in a stainless-steel bowl and mixing well with anchovies and garlic. Slowly whisk in oil and, when thick, stir in lemon juice.

Grill bacon until crisp. Poach eggs in barely simmering water for 2 minutes. Cut the whole lettuce in half lengthwise and wash and drain thoroughly. Drizzle lightly with olive oil and place, cut-side-down, in a pan or on a grill for just 1 minute. Turn over and cook for 1 minute more.

To serve, place each lettuce half in a large bowl, sprinkle with broken-up bacon, poached egg, drizzle with dressing and top with the shaved parmesan. Serve with grissini sticks.

Choose a riesling, preferably the excellent Vasse Felix label.

INGREDIENTS

2 rashers bacon

2 eggs

1 cos lettuce

2 tablespoons olive oil

dressing

2 egg yolks

2 anchovy fillets, chopped

3 cloves garlic, crushed

3/4 cup (190ml/6fl oz) olive oil

juice of half a lemon

to serve

shaved parmesan

grissini sticks

This recipe is based on one from Brisbane Masterclass, an annual weekend gourmet gab fest, but I serve it hot, not cold as originally intended.

INGREDIENTS   Serves 4–6

4 cups (1 litre/1¾ pints)
chicken consomme or
clear chicken stock

2 stems lemon grass,
sliced into rounds

4 kaffir lime leaves

8 black peppercorns

1 sprig of mint

24 green medium king prawns,
peeled and deveined

Bring stock to the boil with all the flavouring ingredients, except prawns. Reduce heat to a simmer and add prawns. Poach for 2–3 minutes, or until prawns are just cooked through and opaque. Serve immediately in bowls with some of the broth.

Choose a semillon for a sensational pairing.

prawns poached in lemon grass broth

fish with rocket and anchovy butter

This is another recipe I developed for my 'Fast & Fabulous' column in **Australian Good Taste**. I love it as a simple way of jazzing up a piece of plain white fish and for the wonderful bright green the butter goes as it melts on the fish.

Serves 6

To prepare rocket and anchovy butter, chop rocket and anchovies in a food processor. Add butter and process until smooth. Place on plastic wrap or foil and roll up into a thick sausage shape. Chill until required.

To cook fish, melt butter with oil in a large frying pan over high heat. Pan-fry fish fillets for only about 3 minutes each side, until cooked through and opaque. Lift from the pan and flip over so that the side that was cooked second is uppermost on the plate. Place each piece of fish on a simple bed of rocket leaves, top with a slice or two of rocket and anchovy butter and serve immediately.

Note: If there's any rocket and anchovy butter left over, it will keep indefinitely in the freezer. Zap up chicken, potato or any type of fish simply by topping with a slice of this tangy butter.

An unoaked or lightly oaked chardonnay will balance the butter in this dish, without its taste becoming bitter because of the rocket.

INGREDIENTS

1 tablespoon butter

1 tablespoon olive oil

6 large skinless fish fillets (e.g. snapper, gemfish or ling)

rocket leaves (arugula), to serve

rocket and anchovy butter

8 large leaves rocket

5 anchovy fillets

100g (3^1/$_2$oz) butter

char-grilled chicken breast with coriander and cashew nut pesto

INGREDIENTS

4 chicken breast fillets

2 red capsicum (red pepper), seeded and cut into large, flat pieces

2–4 baby eggplant (aubergine), depending on size, sliced lengthwise into 1cm (½in) slices

2 large zucchini (courgette), sliced lengthwise into 1cm (½in) slices

1 punnet baby corn

olive oil

pesto

2 cloves garlic

½ red chilli

½ bunch coriander (cilantro)

200g (6½oz) salted, roasted cashews

salt and freshly ground pepper

⅔ cup (160ml/5fl oz) extra virgin olive oil

This pesto is quite subtle and makes a pleasant change from traditional basil and pinenut pesto. It will keep well under a layer of olive oil in the refrigerator.

Serves 4

Make pesto first by finely chopping garlic, chilli and coriander in a food processor. Add cashews and salt and pepper to taste and process until finely chopped. With motor running, slowly pour in oil.

Brush chicken and vegetables with oil. Place chicken and capsicum on char-grill first; add the other vegetables a few minutes later. Turn only once, after 5–8 minutes, so grill marks remain clear. Cook on second side for 5–8 minutes more.

To serve, layer the vegetables on 4 plates, top each with a chicken breast and a good dollop of pesto.

Choose a wooded wine, such as a chardonnay or wooded semillon, to complement the smoky character of this and other food from the char-grill.

smoked chicken salad

Choose a naturally smoked chicken with excellent flavour. This versatile product is great on the barbecue, in school lunches, with pasta, potato salad or, as here, the focus of a salad.

Serves 2

One good-sized smoked chicken breast will be enough for two people. Slice and serve on a plate with vegetables, such as those listed, at room temperature. Make dressing by thinning chilli sauce with oil and vinegar. Season to taste and drizzle over salad.

Select an unwooded chardonnay or semillon or, because the chilli is only mild, a chenin blanc or marsanne. Wooded chardonnay and chilli are not good friends, but riesling is always a safe choice.

INGREDIENTS

1 large smoked chicken breast

choice of salad vegetables
e.g. avocado, blanched beans,
broccoli, sun-dried capsicum
and canned, drained chickpeas

dressing

2 tablespoons Thai sweet
chilli sauce

2 tablespoons olive oil
or extra virgin olive oil

2 teaspoons white vinegar

salt and freshly ground pepper

Asian-style roast pork salad

INGREDIENTS

375g (12oz) Chinese roast pork

1 bunch watercress, broken into sprigs

3 cups bean sprouts

1/2 small Chinese cabbage, shredded

1 Spanish onion, finely sliced

dressing

2 cloves garlic, crushed

5cm (2in) piece ginger, grated

2 teaspoons Thai sweet chilli sauce

1/3 cup (80ml/2$\frac{1}{2}$fl oz) low-salt soy sauce

1/3 cup (80ml/2$\frac{1}{2}$fl oz) peanut oil

2 tablespoons lime juice

2 teaspoons sugar

good pinch Chinese 5 spice

I love roast pork or suckling pig the way the Chinese do it – my family are all big fans of the crackling and I buy roast pork, for a treat, from my local Asian supermarket. Combined here with salad ingredients, it makes a wonderful dish with great texture and flavour contrasts – and, best of all, it takes hardly any effort.

Serves 6–8

Combine dressing ingredients and set aside. Have pork warm or at room temperature – it can be reheated in a moderate oven, 180°–190°C (350°–375°F) Gas Mark 4, so the crackling stays crisp. Toss all salad ingredients together in a large salad bowl and pour dressing over. Serve immediately with the pork.

For this dish choose a sauvignon blanc, a dry style of gewurztraminer or a riesling.

scotch steak

This dish is so simple it almost cooks itself.

Serves 4

Heat butter or oil and seal steaks over high heat for about 2 minutes each side, or until brown. Reduce heat to medium/high and pan-fry to required 'doneness'. (This will depend on the thickness of the steaks. For a thick steak, 3 minutes each side will be medium/rare.) Remove from pan and keep warm. Add whisky to warm pan and flame it (if you like). Add cream, stock and mushrooms, bring to the boil and simmer, stirring occasionally, until the sauce has been reduced by about half. Add mustard, salt and pepper to taste. Pour over steaks and serve with a green salad.

Choose a cabernet sauvignon – its firm tannins go very well with the mushrooms and cream.

INGREDIENTS

1 tablespoon butter or olive oil, for frying

4 x 220g (7oz) steaks

$1/3$ cup (80ml/$2^1/_2$fl oz) Scotch whisky

$1^1/_4$ cups (300ml/$1/_2$ pint) cream

$2/3$ cup (160ml/5fl oz) beef stock

125g (4oz) mushrooms, sliced

1 teaspoon coarse-grain mustard

salt and freshly ground pepper

INGREDIENTS

8 lamb loin chops

3/4 cup (190ml/6fl oz) thick Greek-style yoghurt, to serve

marinade

1 small onion, grated

2 teaspoons cumin

freshly ground black pepper

juice of 1 lemon

1/4 cup (60ml/2fl oz) olive oil

potatoes with onion and rosemary

1/4 cup (60ml/2fl oz) olive oil

4 medium potatoes, skin on, sliced thickly

1 onion, sliced

1 1/4 cups (300ml/1/2 pint) beef stock

sprigs of fresh rosemary

tomato sauce

1 tablespoon olive oil

3 ripe red tomatoes, peeled, seeded and chopped

1 long green chilli, seeded and finely chopped

1 clove garlic, crushed

pinch each of salt, sugar and black pepper

1 teaspoon red wine vinegar

A succulent lamb dish inspired by Turkish cooking.

Serves 4

Combine marinade ingredients and lavish over both sides of chops. Marinate for at least 1 hour at room temperature or longer in the refrigerator.

To prepare potatoes, heat oil in a large frying-pan over high heat. Cook potato slices for 1–2 minutes each side. Add onion and cook for 1 minute more. Cover with stock, add rosemary, reduce heat and simmer for 10–15 minutes, or until soft. Top up with stock or water if liquid evaporates too quickly during cooking, but all liquid should have evaporated by the time the potatoes are ready to serve.

Preheat char-grill or griller and cook lamb chops for 3–5 minutes each side, or until cooked to required 'doneness'.

Meanwhile, for the tomato sauce, heat olive oil with tomato, chilli and garlic and cook over high heat, stirring frequently, until thick and sauce-like. Stir in salt, sugar, pepper and vinegar. Set aside.

Serve lamb chops with tomato sauce and a dollop of yoghurt, beside potatoes with onion and rosemary.

Semillon and chambourcin both have a special affinity with tomatoes. Any light style of red wine, or even a shiraz, complements the subtle spicing of this dish.

marinated lamb loin chops with tomato sauce and yoghurt

I'm sure chillies are addictive — they certainly give you the 'feel goods'. The capsaicin in them triggers the brain to produce endorphins, a natural painkiller that promotes a sense of wellbeing and stimulation — the same one athletes experience after passing the pain barrier! I prefer to do it by eating.

Hot 'n' Spicy

The idea for this recipe took my fancy because, while it's hot, it isn't really a curry – an easy way to eat more health-giving fish yet enjoy a punch of flavour. I love the fact that there is no rich sauce; instead, there's a wonderful finish that's almost sour and very refreshing.

barramundi achari

INGREDIENTS

Serves 4

1 tablespoon extra light olive oil

1 onion, sliced

3 red chillies, seeded and chopped

4 barramundi cutlets, about 1kg (2lbs)

2 tomatoes, sliced

$2/3$ cup (160ml/5fl oz) fish stock or water

pinch salt

1 tablespoon lime pickle
(lime is delicious but any other is fine)

juice of 1 large lime or lemon

$1/2$ bunch coriander (cilantro), chopped

to serve

jasmine rice, steamed

Heat oil in a very large pan and cook onion. After 2 minutes add chilli. Move to side of pan, add barramundi cutlets and brown on both sides for 1 or 2 minutes. Add tomato and fish stock and cook for 2 minutes more. Add salt, pickle, lime juice and coriander. Turn the fish over just once, mixing the sauce as you go. Serve with steamed jasmine rice.

Choose a wine with some fruit sweetness, such as riesling, gewurztraminer or grenache, to counteract the spiciness of the chilli.

deep-fried bean curd with chilli sauce

Some time ago I visited Club Med at Cherating, Malaysia. At Kuala Lumpur Airport I was met by friends who took me to a restaurant literally at the end of the runway. This dish so impressed me that I was determined to recreate it. For simplicity, I use a commercial chilli sauce as the base.

Serves 4

Drain tofu, slice and marinate in soy sauce for at least 10 minutes.

To make chilli sauce, heat oil and fry garlic and eschalots until softening. Add chilli sauce, fish sauce, sugar and water and simmer for 1–2 minutes. Taste. If it is too hot, thin with more water.

Heat oil in a saucepan or deep-fryer. Drain bean curd and pat dry on paper towels. Deep-fry bean curd briefly in hot oil. Drain and place on serving dish. Top with sauce and green shallots.

The inside of the bean curd will be wondrously silky and soft, demonstrating why texture is such an important consideration in Asian food.

This is a fiery dish, so choose a gewurztraminer, riesling, sauvignon blanc or pinot noir.

INGREDIENTS

625g (1¼lbs) firm tofu or bean curd

¼ cup (60ml/2fl oz) soy sauce

oil, for deep frying e.g. peanut, grapeseed, extra light olive

chilli sauce

1 tablespoon peanut oil

2 cloves garlic, chopped

2 eschalots, chopped

¾ cup (190ml/6fl oz) chilli sauce

1 tablespoons Thai fish sauce

1 teaspoon sugar

5 tablespoons (100ml/3fl oz) water

to serve

½ bunch green shallots, sliced

2 red chillies, sliced, for garnish

king prawns with harissa sauce

I have twice had the pleasure of judging the Noosa Good Food Awards on Queensland's Sunshine Coast. Chef Phil Mitchell created the awards lunch one year, a wonderful succession of platters coming to the centre of each table. He served his prawns in a jacket of besan (chickpea flour). This is my fast and easy version with Phil's distinctive harissa sauce.

INGREDIENTS

48 (2kg/4lb 8oz) green medium king prawns

1–2 tablespoons olive oil

harissa sauce

1 red capsicum

1 whole bulb garlic

1/2 cup (125ml/4fl oz) sweet ground paprika

6 small red chillies, seeded and roughly chopped

1 bunch coriander (cilantro)

1 teaspoon pure saffron powder

2 teaspoons salt

1 teaspoon cayenne pepper

juice of 2 limes

1 cup (250ml/8fl oz) olive oil

Serves 8

To make harissa sauce, roast capsicum and garlic in a moderate oven, 180°–190°C (350°–375°F) Gas Mark 4, until capsicum skin is blackened and blistered. For the last few minutes put paprika in oven to toast. Place capsicum in a plastic bag (this makes peeling easier) until cool enough to handle. Peel garlic and capsicum and remove seeds. Process in a food processor, progressively adding chilli, coriander, capsicum, garlic, paprika, saffron, salt, cayenne pepper, lime juice and olive oil, until smooth. Refrigerate, covered, until ready to use. This allows the flavours to develop. Keeps well in the refrigerator under a layer of olive oil.

Peel and devein prawns. Pan-fry in a little olive oil, turning after a minute or so. This will take only about 4 minutes altogether. Don't overcook. Serve hot, warm or at room temperature with a dab of harissa sauce and a tumble of salad greens.

Pinot noir or grenache are particularly well suited to this roasted, red harissa. They can handle the spice and are robust enough for the sauce. Alternatively, try a riesling or gewurztraminer.

thai-style red curry of chicken livers

Thai curries have become firm favourites. Here, chicken livers make a wonderful variation — a suggestion by photographer Michael Cook. If you don't like offal, substitute lamb or beef strips.

Serves 6

Trim chicken livers. Heat oil in a wok or large saucepan over high heat and cook garlic, ginger, curry paste and chilli for 1 to 2 minutes, or until fragrant. Add chicken livers and toss to coat in the curry paste. (If your pan is not large, it may be better to do this in batches, combining at the end.) Cook gently, turning frequently until chicken livers are browned on the outside. Add coconut milk, lime leaves, palm sugar, lime juice and fish sauce. Reduce heat and simmer 5–10 minutes. Garnish with coriander leaves and serve with jasmine rice.

Choose a full-bodied shiraz to accompany a red curry. Cool-climate shiraz can have a peppery quality, similar to the spiciness of the curry, while warm-climate shiraz tends to be full and rich, complementing the curry like a chutney.

INGREDIENTS

1kg (2lbs) chicken livers

2 tablespoons vegetable oil, e.g. peanut

3 cloves garlic, crushed

2.5cm (1in) piece fresh ginger, grated

2 tablespoons red curry paste

3–4 red chillies (optional), seeded and finely chopped

2 cups (500ml/16fl oz) coconut milk

3 fresh or dried Kaffir lime leaves, soaked in a little boiling water (or substitute rind of 1 lime for the leaves)

1 tablespoon palm sugar (or brown sugar)

juice of 1 lime

1 tablespoon Thai fish sauce

1/4 cup fresh coriander (cilantro) leaves, for garnish

spicy pork stir-fry with noodles

When I went to Bangkok and saw through the Asian Home Gourmet factory, I was astounded by its cleanliness and calm and the quality of fresh product used to make the pastes. Curry pastes are a boon to the home cook who does not have the time to roast and grind spices. It's a great way to enjoy authentic flavours. But we Australians are great adaptors and so I have used tom yum paste not for soup, but in a stir-fry. It gives a delicious and unusual flavour.

INGREDIENTS

Serves 4

625g (1¼lbs) lean diced pork

30–60g (1–2oz) red curry paste

30–60g (1–2oz) tom yum soup paste

peanut oil

½ cup sliced green shallots

½ cup (125ml/4fl oz) chicken stock

½ cup peanuts, preferably dry-roasted

½ bunch coriander (cilantro), chopped

to serve

egg noodles

Mix pork with red curry paste and tom yum paste and leave to marinate, preferably for 1–2 hours.

Heat oil in a wok until very hot and, making sure your exhaust fan is on, quickly sear and begin to cook pork, in 2 batches, for 2 minutes each batch. Return it all to the wok and add green shallots. Cook about 1 minute longer, but don't let it burn. Add stock and cook until pork is cooked through. Throw in peanuts and coriander and stir through. Serve pork over egg noodles.

Note: This dish is HOT! To reduce the heat, decrease the quantity of spice paste you use.

Choose a wine with fruit sweetness to counteract the heat of the chilli, perhaps a sauvignon blanc, gewurztraminer, riesling, pinot noir or grenache.

Nam jim is a versatile accompaniment for plain grilled chicken or lamb. It is sensational with quail. This dish was inspired by one created by Michael Voumard of the Botanic Dining Room, Adelaide.

spiced quail with nam jim

Serves 6 as an entree or part of a larger meal, 3 as a main course

Combine all marinade ingredients in a large bowl and rub all over the quail. Marinate for at least 1 hour.

Grill quail for about 10 minutes each side, taking care not to burn. Alternatively, cook in a hot oven, 220°–230°C (450°–475°F) Gas Mark 6, for about 20 minutes, or on the barbecue. Rest quail in a warm place for about 5 minutes.

To prepare nam jim, combine coriander, chilli, eschalots, garlic and palm sugar in a food processor, then blend in lime juice and fish sauce. Serve quail on a banana leaf (optional) with rice noodles and nam jim.

Choose a soft style of red wine, such as pinot noir or grenache.

INGREDIENTS

6 quail

marinade

1/4 cup (60ml/2fl oz) kecap manis (sweet Indonesian soy sauce)

1 tablespoon Thai fish sauce

2 tablespoons rice wine vinegar or mirin

2 tablespoons ground coriander (cilantro)

1 teaspoon ground cumin

5 pieces star anise

1 bunch coriander, leaves

nam jim

4 large coriander, roots

3 red chillies, seeded

15 eschalots

4 cloves garlic

155g (5oz) palm sugar (or brown sugar)

3/4 cup (190ml/6fl oz) fresh lime juice (4–5 limes)

1/4 cup (60ml/2fl oz) fish sauce

'Summer time and the living is easy …' goes the song. This is minimal-fuss, minimal-heat food for those long summer days.

Cool Food

tapenade

Provence is the home of this famous olive and caper spread. It takes its name from the French word for capers, but it relies more on olives than capers. Although widely available, it is very easy to make.

INGREDIENTS   Serves 4

1 cup (150g/5oz) black olives, stoned

pinch of thyme

2 anchovy fillets

1–2 tablespoons capers (depending on personal taste), rinsed

freshly ground black pepper

2 teaspoons lemon juice

2 tablespoons olive oil

optional extras

1 red chilli, finely chopped

1 tablespoon Continental parsley

pinch of mustard

Combine olives, thyme, anchovies, capers, pepper and any of the optional items in a food processor. Add lemon juice and then slowly add olive oil to make a thick paste. It can be as smooth or as chunky as you like. Keeps well in the refrigerator under a layer of olive oil.

Note: Tapenade is wonderful spread on bread, Melba toast, bruschetta or focaccia or with anything char-grilled. It also makes a wonderful reduction sauce to serve with veal or beef. Reduce 2 cups (500ml) beef stock, 1 cup (250ml) wine, $1/3$ cup (80ml) cream and 1–2 tablespoons tapenade over high heat until sauce is thick.

Choose any of the Italian varietals with a tapenade, which is both salty and bitter. This tends to accentuate fruit sweetness in wine. Alternatively, serve a pinot noir, a grenache/shiraz or perhaps a chilled fino sherry.

I love the light, transparent look of cellophane noodles. This salad doesn't take long to make and can be assembled, except for the peanuts, several hours ahead. It's very cooling in hot weather and can be given more substance by adding shredded chicken, pork or prawns at the last minute.

glass noodle salad

Serves 4–6

Soak cellophane noodles in warm water for 10 minutes. Drain. Combine lime juice, fish sauce and chilli sauce (an easy way is to shake well in a screw-top jar). Pour over drained noodles and toss to mix through.

Add onion, green shallots, coriander and mint and toss through gently. Just before serving, toss peanuts through.

For this dish choose a fragrant gewurztraminer to accompany this aromatic, spicy dish.

INGREDIENTS

125g (4oz) mung or green bean vermicelli (cellophane noodles)

2 tablespoons lime or lemon juice

1 tablespoon Thai fish sauce

2 tablespoons Thai sweet chilli sauce

1 large Spanish onion, sliced

3 tablespoons green shallots, chopped

2 tablespoons fresh coriander (cilantro), finely chopped

2 tablespoons fresh mint leaves, finely chopped

90g (3oz) peanuts (good quality, shelled and lightly salted)

My version is inspired by a very popular Thai recipe.
The pawpaw must be very green – if your fruiterer doesn't
regularly stock them, order one in. To serve as a light
meal, add 250g (8oz) small prawns or shredded
chicken and roasted peanuts at the last minute.

green pawpaw salad

INGREDIENTS

Serves 6–8 as an accompaniment

1 medium green pawpaw (papaya),
about 750g (1½ lbs)

1 clove garlic, finely chopped

2.5cm (1in) piece ginger, grated

2 spring onions, finely sliced

1 red or green chilli, seeded and chopped

¼ cup (60ml/2fl oz) lime juice (from 1–2 limes)

2 tablespoons Thai fish sauce

1 tablespoon palm sugar
(or brown sugar)

Peel, seed and julienne pawpaw. (A Japanese grater does an excellent job, or shave with a vegetable peeler and cut into long fine strips.) Mix with garlic, ginger, spring onion and chilli.

Combine remaining ingredients, stirring until sugar has dissolved, and pour over pawpaw mixture.

The acid in this dish makes matching a wine difficult. Try a sauvignon blanc.

INGREDIENTS

6 whole baby snapper
(1 per person), scaled and cleaned

juice of 1 lemon

$1/2$ cup (125ml/4fl oz) dry white wine

coriander (cilantro) leaves, for garnish

tomato and lime salsa

1 large or 2 small tomatoes,
about 125g (4oz), seeded and diced,

$1/2$ green capsicum (green pepper),
about 60g (2oz), seeded and diced,

$1/2$ red capsicum (red pepper),
about 60g (2oz), seeded and diced,

$1/2$ medium Spanish onion, chopped

$1/2$ bunch coriander (cilantro),
chopped

juice and rind of 1 lime

few drops Tabasco sauce

1 tablespoon balsamic vinegar

$1/4$ cup (60ml/2fl oz) olive oil

salt and freshly ground pepper

Whole fish is quite a different proposition from fillets. It is more economical, easier to present well and retains moisture and flavour beautifully – as long as you and your guests can cope with the bones.

Serves 6

Preheat oven to moderate, 180°–190°C (350°–375°F) Gas Mark 4. Cut fins and tails off fish. Slash each through to the bone on one side, place in a baking dish and sprinkle with lemon juice and/or white wine. Cover with foil and bake for 10–12 minutes (when fish is cooked it will be opaque and flake easily away from the bones). Alternatively, if you are a little daunted by whole fish, pan-fry or steam snapper or bream fillets.

Meanwhile, combine salsa ingredients.

To serve, spoon salsa over fish, especially where it has been slashed so that the flavours can be absorbed. Garnish with coriander leaves.

Choose a riesling or semillon for this fresh-flavoured dish with only a hint of heat.

whole baby snapper with tomato and lime salsa

grilled eye of lamb loin with onion and parsley salad

Australian lamb is absolutely my favourite meat – juicy, succulent and sweet. It also adapts well to the flavours of many different nations – here it is given a Turkish twist.

INGREDIENTS   Serves 4

2 eye of lamb loin
(or lamb backstraps)

8 pieces pocket pitta, flat pitta or lavash bread, to serve

marinade

1 tablespoon tomato paste

1 teaspoon harissa or hot chilli paste

2 cloves garlic, crushed

1/2 teaspoon mixed spice

1/2 teaspoon cumin

freshly ground black pepper

1/4 cup (60ml/2fl oz) olive oil

onion and parsley salad

2 Spanish onions, thinly sliced

sea salt

1/2 cup chopped parsley

2 tablespoons chopped mint

Combine marinade ingredients in a flat glass or ceramic dish. Cut each loin downwards into about 16 thin slices. Add to marinade, stir to coat meat and refrigerate, preferably 8–12 hours. Soak 8 bamboo skewers in cold water for an hour before using, to prevent scorching.

Make salad by rubbing onion slices with sea salt and standing for 5 minutes. Rinse and drain onions thoroughly. Toss with parsley and mint.

Thread meat on skewers, allowing 4 pieces per skewer. Preheat char-grill or griller and cook kebabs quickly, no more than 1–2 minutes each side. Heat pitta bread at the same time.

To serve, split the bread or lay the larger slices flat. Place 2 tablespoons or more of salad in centre of each piece and push meat off skewers onto bread. Meat from 2 skewers makes 1 serving. Fold bread over and serve immediately.

Choose either a white wine such as sauvignon blanc, or a red such as pinot noir, grenache or a rose style to balance the mild spicing in the lamb and salad.

lamb with tarator sauce

Tarator is one of those new/old sauces, a long-time favourite in northern Africa but discovered much more recently in the West. It holds up well in the refrigerator, tightly covered, so can be made beforehand.

Serves 6

To prepare the sauce, grind walnuts coarsely in a food processor, taking care to retain some texture. Soak bread in cold water and immediately squeeze dry. Add bread to walnuts with remaining sauce ingredients and process just until combined. The sauce should be thick and slightly chunky.

For the salad, combine salad ingredients and toss with a vinaigrette made from the olive oil and lemon juice.

Pan-fry lamb steaks over high heat for no more than 2 minutes each side. Serve topped with Tarator Sauce and Shepherd's Salad as an accompaniment.

Just for a change, serve a chilled sherry or Spanish wine with this sauce, which has a wonderful nutty texture. Alternatively, serve a chardonnay or almost any red wine.

INGREDIENTS

3 lamb round roasts, cut into steaks

olive oil

tarator sauce

125g (4oz) walnuts

1 slice white bread

2 cloves garlic, crushed

2 tablespoons lemon juice

1/3 – 1/2 cup (80–125ml/ 21/2 – 4fl oz) olive oil

pinch of salt

shepherd's salad

2 large ripe red tomatoes, cubed

2 Lebanese cucumbers, cubed

2 white onions, diced

1 bunch parsley, finely chopped

1/4 cup (60ml/2fl oz) olive oil

1 tablespoon lemon juice

I came across this dish, which is as surprising as it is simple, in Portugal. It was served by an olive oil producer in a region well known for both honey and olive oil. Just choose varieties with a flavour you love.

oranges with honey and olive oil

Serves 8

Peel oranges, remove pith and slice oranges into rounds. Arrange on a plate and drizzle with honey and olive oil. Sprinkle with pepper, if desired. Serve at the beginning or end of a meal, as a snack, or even as a salad or palate refresher during the meal.

As a palate refresher, this is better without wine.

INGREDIENTS

6 oranges

2 tablespoons honey, approx.

2 tablespoons olive oil, approx.

freshly ground black pepper, optional

watermelon with iced gin

I always keep a bottle of gin in the freezer – well, a girl never knows when she might need a martini. It makes a wonderful accompaniment to watermelon. Iced vodka can be substituted and gives a completely different taste sensation.

This is so simple it scarcely needs a recipe. Just cut the watermelon into wedges and serve on a plate beside a shot glass of iced gin. It is imperative that the gin is of a very good quality, such as Tanqueray, Bombay Sapphire or Gordons. Dip watermelon wedges into the gin if you're feeling really decadent.

Food is as much about texture and sensation as it is about aroma and taste. These recipes are sensuous — use them wisely.

Succulent and Sexy

INGREDIENTS

24 scallops on the shell

2.5cm (1in) knob ginger,
finely chopped

3 green shallots, finely chopped

1 tablespoon kecap manis
(sweet Indonesian soy sauce)

1 tablespoon water

1 teaspoon sesame oil

Chinese restaurants serve scallops steamed in this way. I developed this recipe for a seafood class that focussed on seafood and semillon. It was a winner.

scallops steamed with ginger, shallots and sesame

Serves 4

Place the scallops in Chinese steamer baskets. Combine the remaining ingredients and spoon over the scallops. Steam over boiling water for about 2 minutes, or until the scallops are opaque and just cooked. Serve immediately.

For this dish choose a semillon with this dish or serve a chilled fino sherry for a different approach.

Perhaps not a classic risotto but a great way of using smoked salmon off-cuts. Light sour cream or cream and lemon juice could be substituted for crème fraîche.

smoked salmon 'risotto'

Serves 4

Heat stock to simmering point (the microwave is handy for this). Melt butter over medium heat in a large saucepan, add onion and cook until softened. Add rice and stir thoroughly to coat the grains with butter. Toast rice gently for 1–2 minutes, add wine and stir until absorbed. Season with salt and pepper to taste.

Add hot stock, 1/2 cup (125ml) at a time, stirring frequently and allowing each addition of stock to be absorbed before adding the next. When almost cooked and only a little stock remains, stir through all the asparagus, except the tips. Stir the tips through with the last of the hot stock. Cook until rice is tender and the risotto is soft and creamy. Carefully stir through salmon and crème fraîche and serve immediately.

Microwave method: (All cooking is done on high.) Heat butter, uncovered, in a large microwave-safe container for 1 minute. Add onion and cook for 2 minutes. Stir in rice and cook for 1 minute. Add wine and cook 1 minute more. Add stock and cook, covered, for 16 minutes. Add asparagus stems and cook for 2 minutes before adding asparagus tips and cooking for a final 3 minutes. Stir salmon and crème fraîche through carefully, rest for a couple of minutes and serve.

Choose a sauvignon blanc, especially the herbaceous New Zealand style, or a lean, elegant chardonnay. Either marries well with the slight acidity imparted by the crème fraîche.

INGREDIENTS

3 cups (750ml/24fl oz) or more fish or chicken stock

60g (2oz) butter

1 medium onion, chopped

315g (10oz) Arborio rice

1/2 cup (125ml/4fl oz) dry white wine

salt and freshly ground black pepper

1 bunch asparagus, cut into 5cm (2in) lengths

90g (3oz) smoked salmon pieces

2 tablespoons crème fraîche

INGREDIENTS

¹/₄ cup wakame

250g (8oz) fresh coriander
(cilantro) tagliolini

1 bunch asparagus, cut in half

5 spring onions, halved

1 tablespoon light olive oil

1 teaspoon sesame oil

250g (8oz) fresh shiitake mushrooms, sliced

2 cloves garlic, finely chopped

2 green chillies, seeded and chopped

small knob fresh ginger

24 green medium king prawns, shelled

¹/₃ cup (80ml/2¹/₂fl oz) Thai fish sauce

juice of 2 limes

salt and freshly ground pepper

1¹/₂ cups (375ml/12fl oz) fish stock
(heated in microwave or saucepan)

1 tablespoon kecap manis
(sweet Indonesian soy sauce)

A trip to Tasmania showcased the variety and quality of its produce to advantage. On King Island, I was interested to see seaweed being dried for many uses. Wakame, or dried flakes, are readily available and make an unusual and delicious addition to seafood dishes, especially those with an Asian flavour.

Serves 6

Soak wakame in hot water for 15 minutes (not absolutely necessary but I prefer to). Bring a large pot of salted water to the boil and cook tagliolini following directions on packet. Add asparagus to the pasta for last 2 minutes.

Meanwhile, cook spring onion over medium heat in some light olive oil flavoured with sesame oil. Add mushrooms, garlic, chilli and ginger and cook for 1–2 minutes. Add prawns and cook only about 1 minute longer, or until they are opaque.

Drain pasta and asparagus. Return to the drained saucepan and add prawn mixture, fish sauce, lime juice, salt and pepper to taste, hot fish stock and kecap manis. Toss together and serve immediately.

Why not choose sake with these Japanese flavours?

prawns with coriander tagliolini

It's pretty amazing in a new country like Australia to think that a mustard-making company could be 250 years old. Well, the French company Maille (pronounced my) is! The range of mustards continues to evolve and there are some terrific new ones. In celebration, I developed a couple of recipes using two of my favourites.

Serves 6

Cook pasta in plenty of boiling, salted water, following directions on packet. Meanwhile, heat oil or butter in a frying pan and sear tuna steaks over high heat until brown on both sides. Reduce heat to medium and add mushrooms to pan. When tuna is cooked as desired (I like mine rare, which takes only about 2 minutes more) remove both tuna and mushrooms to a warm plate. Add mustard, stock and cream to the pan and increase heat to high. Boil vigorously for 1–2 minutes, or until thickened and reduced.

When pasta is cooked, throw spinach leaves into the saucepan with it. Drain immediately. Serve a mound of pasta and spinach on each plate, surrounded with oyster mushrooms, top with tuna and finally the delicious sauce.

Choose one of the Rhone varietals. Blends of grenache, shiraz and mourvedre go well with the Mediterranean flavours here.

INGREDIENTS

500g (1lb) squid ink pasta
 or other pasta of your choice

1–2 tablespoons olive oil or butter

6 tuna steaks

250g (8oz) oyster mushrooms

2 tablespoons Maille Provençale
 mustard with garlic and red peppers
 (or other strong-flavoured mustard)

$2/3$ cup (160ml/5fl oz) fish
 or chicken stock

$1/4$ cup (60ml/2fl oz) cream

$1/2$ bunch English spinach leaves

tuna with provençale mustard sauce

wild mushroom pasta

INGREDIENTS

500g (1lb) rigatoni

125g (4oz) black fungus

125g (4oz) button mushrooms

125g (4oz) shiitake mushrooms

155g (5oz) shimeji mushrooms

90g (3oz) butter

1 onion, chopped

1 clove garlic, crushed

$1^{1}/_{4}$ cups (300ml/$^{1}/_{2}$ pint) cream

$^{3}/_{4}$ cup (190ml/6fl oz) chicken or vegetable stock

salt and freshly ground pepper

125g (4oz) enoki mushrooms

$^{1}/_{2}$ bunch garlic chives, with flowers, if in season

I just love the many varieties of mushroom and fungi now available fresh. This is a basic recipe for a mushroom ragout that can be served in a little pot or ramekin with crusty bread as an entree, or with meat or pasta as a main course.

Serves 6 as an entree, 4 as a main course

Bring 4 litres salted water to a rolling boil. Add rigatoni and cook following directions on packet. Wipe mushrooms clean with a kitchen towel or soft cloth and slice, leaving some small mushrooms whole for variety. Melt all but 1 tablespoon butter in a frying pan over medium heat. Soften the onion, adding garlic after 1–2 minutes. When onion is wilted but not brown, add all the mushrooms, except the enoki. Cook until almost cooked through, then stir in cream and stock. Bring to the boil and simmer. Season with salt and pepper to taste. Cook enoki mushrooms in remaining butter in a separate pan.

Drain pasta and put into a large warmed bowl. Pour the sauce over and toss pasta through. The sauce will cook more as it clings to the hot pasta. Garnish with enoki mushrooms and snip garlic chives over the top.

Choose a flavoursome wine, such as chardonnay, with rich, creamy foods.

asparagus on garlicky bean puree with crisp pancetta

Asparagus is the most wonderful vegetable. To prepare, simply bend at the end and it will snap off in exactly the right place. Beans and pulses are very good for us and we don't use them often enough – pureed they are wonderful with all sorts of things.

Serves 4

Melt butter in a small saucepan and cook garlic gently over low heat. Add beans, including their liquid (see Note), and heat through. Mash or puree in food processor. Grill or dry-fry pancetta in a non-stick pan.

Meanwhile, bring plenty of water to the boil in a frying-pan or asparagus steamer and cook asparagus for a few minutes, or until cooked but still firm. (You could also use your microwave.) Drain.

To serve, place some bean puree on 4 plates, top with asparagus, crisp pancetta and a drizzle of olive oil.

Note: Taste the liquid in the canned beans – sometimes it has food acid in it which is not very palatable. If so, drain and rinse beans and substitute water or stock for the liquid.

Choose the classic wine to serve with asparagus – sauvignon blanc – to highlight its crisp herbaceousness.

INGREDIENTS

1 tablespoon butter

2 cloves garlic

310g (10oz) canned white beans e.g. cannelini, butter beans

4 slices pancetta

2 bunches asparagus

extra virgin olive oil

This is a second recipe I developed to commemorate the 250th anniversary of Maille mustards. Dijonnaise is a blend of Dijon, seeded mustard and mayonnaise, delicious on its own or a great shortcut to a sauce.

spatchcock dijonnaise

Serves 6

Preheat oven to moderately hot, 200°–210°C (400°–425°F) Gas Mark 5. Combine equal quantities of mustard and butter. Using your fingers, force about 2 tablespoons of this mixture under the skin and over the breast of each spatchcock. Place in oven with 1 whole bulb of garlic per person – slice off the top before cooking to reveal the garlic cloves.

Meanwhile, bake, steam or microwave pumpkin until very soft. Mash with butter, salt and pepper, adding a little more butter or cream, milk or stock if it is too stiff.

After 20 minutes, check if spatchcock are cooked by piercing the thickest part of thighs. If juices run clear, they are cooked. Otherwise return to the oven for another 5–10 minutes. Remove with the garlic to a warm plate to rest, upending the spatchcock so that any juices inside run into the baking dish. Boil the contents of the baking pan over high heat while you cook some Italian beans in salted boiling water for a few minutes.

INGREDIENTS

6 tablespoons Dijonnaise mustard

120g (4oz) softened butter

6 spatchcock or poussin (baby chicken)

6 whole bulbs of garlic

30 large, flat Italian beans

pumpkin puree

1kg (2lbs) butternut pumpkin

2 tablespoons butter

salt and freshly ground pepper

To serve, place a mound of pumpkin puree on each plate. Place the beans, spatchcock and garlic (which will now be sweet and soft and squeeze easily out of its skin) on the plate and drizzle with pan juices.

Choose a lighter style of red wine, such as pinot noir, an Italian varietal, or a chardonnay to balance the buttery flavours of this dish, with just a little kick from the mustard.

Sometimes the occasion demands that you spend a little more time and take a little more trouble — though still the fast and fabulous way.

Indulgences

This is a real spring menu using seasonal produce: asparagus, Snowy Mountains trout and Australia's own native nut, the macadamia.

trout with macadamia nuts

INGREDIENTS   Serves 4

4 plate-size trout, cleaned and scaled

seasoned flour

30g (1oz) butter

2 tablespoons oil

155g (5oz) unroasted, unsalted macadamia nuts or pieces

2 tablespoons parsley, chopped

juice of 2 lemons

2 bunches asparagus

Dredge trout with seasoned flour. Heat butter and oil in a frying pan and cook trout for 4–5 minutes. Turn over and cook 4–5 minutes more, or until fish is opaque and beginning to flake when tested. Transfer to a warm platter.

Add macadamias to pan and cook until golden. Add parsley and lemon juice and cook 1 minute more, reducing the liquid to a glaze.

Meanwhile, cook asparagus in a steamer, in the microwave, or in salted boiling water.

Remove skin of trout, if you wish (it slides off quite easily). Nap with the sauce and serve immediately with asparagus.

Choose a light fresh wine, such as a sauvignon blanc, a classic three-grape white blend, or a semillon, or even a sparkling wine.

Nearly every good cook treasures a version of this recipe.
This is my special one – I hope you like it.

prawn risotto with saffron

Serves 6 as an entree, 4 as a main course

Bring fish stock to the boil either in a saucepan or in the microwave.
Infuse saffron threads in stock.

Heat oil in a heavy-based pan and cook onion, garlic and chilli until soft. Add
rice and stir to coat with oil. Add wine, stir and cook until absorbed. Now begin
to add simmering stock, about 1/2 cup (125ml/4fl oz) at a time. It is imperative
that the stock is at simmering point when it is added to the rice. Stir well after
each addition and let the rice absorb the liquid before adding more.

When the rice is almost cooked and risotto is creamy, add prawns and basil.
Keep stirring until prawns are cooked, about 3 minutes. Season to taste with salt
and pepper. Stir in butter to finish and serve as soon as it has melted.

Microwave method: (For half quantity – full quantity will require a little
longer cooking.) All cooking done on high.

Heat oil and onion in a large microwave-proof dish, uncovered, for 2 minutes,
add garlic and chilli and cook for 1 minute more. Add rice, stir to coat with
oil, and cook, uncovered for 1 minute. Add wine, stir and cook for 2 minutes
more, or until absorbed. Add all the stock and the saffron to the dish. Cover
and cook for 12 minutes. Add prawns and basil and cook for 3 minutes
more. Season to taste with salt and pepper. Stir in butter to finish and
serve as soon as it has melted.

Note: Make a stack of about 10 basil leaves, roll up tightly into
a cigar shape and slice very finely across the roll. Repeat with
remaining leaves. This is called a chiffonade.

Choose a semillon or pinot noir as the ideal partner for this risotto.

INGREDIENTS

4 cups (1 litre/1 3/4 pints)
chicken or fish stock

1 teaspoon saffron threads

1/2 cup (125ml/4fl oz) olive oil

1 onion, finely chopped

2 teaspoons garlic, crushed

2 chillies, seeded
and finely chopped

345g (11oz) Arborio rice

3/4 cup (190ml/6fl oz)
white wine

18 large or 24–30 smaller
green prawns, shelled and
deveined

1/2 bunch basil, leaves only,
cut into a chiffonnade (see Note)

sea salt and freshly ground
black pepper

60g (2oz) butter

crisp-skinned salmon with multicoloured capsicum

I just love the sensation of something that's crisp on the outside yet still moist and soft inside, be it meat or fish. Ocean trout fillets with the skin on could be substituted for the salmon. For a winning combination, team it with caper mashed potatoes.

INGREDIENTS

6 portions salmon fillet, skin-on

plain flour

30g (1oz) butter

2 tablespoons extra virgin olive oil

3 or more different coloured capsicum (peppers), red, yellow, green, purple, seeded and finely sliced

caper mashed potatoes

1kg (2lbs) potatoes, varieties like King Edward, Spunta, Pink Eye, Pontiac

1 cup (250ml/8fl oz) buttermilk

2 cloves garlic, peeled and crushed

salt and freshly ground pepper

2–3 tablespoons drained, rinsed capers

Serves 6

Boil whole potatoes until very soft, drain, skin and mash with buttermilk, garlic and salt and pepper to taste. (Buttermilk gives an unusual flavour and lower fat content but, if you prefer, use about $1/2$ cup/125ml/4fl oz ordinary milk and 110g/4oz butter.) Fold through drained, rinsed capers.

Dip salmon fillets, skin side only, in plain flour. Heat butter and oil in a frying pan over high heat. When foaming, add salmon, skin side down. After 1–2 minutes, add capsicum. Toss to coat with butter/oil mixture, lower heat to medium and cover. After 5 minutes or so, remove lid. The salmon will be pale pink on top but still a rich pink inside and crisp underneath. Serve immediately with caper mashed potatoes and drizzle the pan juices over.

Choose a rich wine, such as a full-bodied chardonnay.

I love mustard, crunchy food and fennel, but fennel is one of those vegetables that often don't seem to have a lot of uses. This recipe successfully combines my three loves.

mustard-crusted chicken breast with fennel and orange

Serves 4

Roll chicken fillets in crushed mustard seeds (if unavailable, crush whole seeds in a blender, pepper mill or with a mortar and pestle). Heat butter and oil in a heavy-based or non-stick pan and pan-fry chicken over high heat for 2 minutes each side to seal. Reduce heat to medium and continue to cook for about 10 minutes, or until cooked through. Remove from pan, increase heat and pour in chicken stock and marmalade. Boil vigorously for several minutes until mixture has a sauce-like consistency.

Meanwhile, prepare fennel by slicing bulbs very finely (a Japanese grater is ideal for the task). Pan-fry with oil and orange rind. Cook only briefly so that the fennel is still rather firm. Right at the end add the orange juice.

To serve, make a bed of fennel on each plate, slice each chicken breast in half and place on top. Throw mint into the sauce and spoon sauce onto chicken breast.

Note: Make a stack of about 10 mint leaves, roll up tightly into a cigar shape and slice very finely across the roll. Repeat with remaining leaves. This is called a chiffonade.

Choose a zesty, fruity wine to best match the flavours of orange and mint, perhaps a riesling, semillon/sauvignon blanc or verdelho.

INGREDIENTS

4 chicken breast fillets

crushed mustard seeds

30g (1oz) butter

1 tablespoon olive oil

$2/3$ cup (160ml/5fl oz) chicken stock

1–2 tablespoons marmalade

2 bulbs fennel

2 tablespoons extra light olive oil

rind and juice of 2 oranges

$1/2$ bunch fresh mint, leaves only, cut into a chiffonnade (see Note)

pork fillet with pistachio and parsley pesto

INGREDIENTS

1 tablespoon olive oil

3 pork fillets, about 1kg (2lbs)

1²/₃ cups (410ml/13fl oz) stock

³/₄ cup (190ml/6fl oz) red wine

pistachio and parsley pesto

200g (6¹/₂oz) pistachio nuts in shells or 100g (3¹/₂oz) pistachio kernels

3 cloves garlic

¹/₂ bunch Continental parsley

pinch salt

75g (2¹/₂oz) fresh parmesan, grated

²/₃ cup (160ml/5fl oz) extra virgin olive oil

Although I am a little tired of traditional pinenut and basil pesto, I love the different flavours made with other herbs and nuts. This one is a particularly good combination that complements lean pork fillet very well.

Serves 6

To prepare pesto, shell pistachios and roast briefly in a moderate oven, 180°–190°C (350°–375°F) Gas Mark 4, or cook on high in the microwave for a few minutes until toasted. This develops the flavour of the nuts. When cool, chop in a food processor. Add garlic, parsley and salt and process to a puree. Add parmesan and process to combine. Slowly pour in the oil, a little at a time, until pesto is smooth and well combined (see Note).

To cook pork, heat olive oil in a frying pan and brown fillets, turning so they brown evenly all over. Either lower the heat and continue to cook more gently until cooked through, or place in a hot oven, 220°–230°C (450°–475°F) Gas Mark 6, for 5–10 minutes. Rest for a few minutes in a warm place before carving diagonally into thick slices.

Pour stock and wine into pan in which pork was cooked. Boil vigorously to reduce. Serve pork with pasta or noodles in individual bowls, pour over reduced stock, top with sliced pork and a dollop of pesto. Alternatively, serve pork and pesto with mashed potato and a green salad.

Note: This amount of pesto will serve 6 comfortably. If there is any left over, it keeps well, covered with olive oil, in the refrigerator.

Choose a full-flavoured wine, such as a chardonnay or oaked semillon, to go with the rich flavours of the pistachio and parsley pesto.

veal with anchovy sauce

Nut of veal is traditionally used for Vitello Tonnato. It is less expensive than the fillet and is ideal cooked in this way. Brief cooking also means less shrinkage so the cut is good value. It is a good idea to rinse the anchovies before you use them to remove extra salt and oil.

Serves 4–6

Preheat oven to hot, 220°–230°C (450°–475°F) Gas Mark 6. Start the sauce by bringing beef stock and wine to the boil in a saucepan and simmering to reduce.

Pour olive oil all over veal, season with pepper and place in a pan. Place garlic cloves around meat and place pan in the oven for 10 minutes to seal. Reduce heat to slow, 150°C (300°F) Gas Mark 2, and cook for another 10 minutes per 500g/1lb 2oz (so for 500g/1lb 2 oz nut cook 10 minutes, for 1kg/2lb 4oz cook 20 minutes). Rest meat in the turned-off oven (or another warm place) for at least 10 minutes.

Meanwhile, make celeriac puree. Peel and dice celeriac and cook in boiling, salted water until tender. Drain. Process in food processor with enough cream to make a thick, mousse-like consistency. (If necessary, place in a heatproof container and cover to keep warm.) Do not add any other seasoning at this stage.

When combined beef stock and wine has been reduced to about 3/4 cup (190ml), remove from heat. Blend with anchovies. Return to the heat and stir in cream. Taste the sauce – it is unlikely to need more salt. After tasting the sauce, you can decide whether or not the celeriac puree needs seasoning. Slice veal, nap with sauce and serve with celeriac mash, steamed English spinach and roasted garlic cloves from around the veal.

Choose a robust red wine with this richly flavoured dish, a cabernet sauvignon, shiraz or Rhone-style blend of grenache, shiraz and mourvedre.

INGREDIENTS

2 tablespoons olive oil

1 nut of veal, from 500g–1kg (1–21bs)

freshly ground black pepper

8 cloves garlic

sauce

1 1/2 cups (375ml/12fl oz) beef stock

3/4 cup (190ml/6fl oz) red wine

6 good quality anchovies, rinsed

2–3 tablespoons thick cream

celeriac puree

2 heads celeriac

2 tablespoons (or more) cream

char-grilled rack of lamb with chickpea puree

OK, so you know I love lamb! I also think that we should use dried beans and pulses more – they can be delicious. I know they take a long time to soak, so if that's a problem, you can use canned chickpeas.

INGREDIENTS

8 racks of lamb with 4 cutlets each, French-trimmed

3 teaspoons cumin

chickpea puree

250g dried chickpeas or 2 cans (400g/13oz) cooked chickpeas

1 tablespoon olive oil

1 onion, sliced

3 cloves garlic

2 cups (500ml/16fl oz) beef stock (for dried chickpea method only)

salt and freshly ground black pepper

Serves 8

Rub trimmed lamb racks with cumin. Cover and refrigerate until ready to cook.

Using dried chickpeas with the 'quick-soak' method: Cover chickpeas with plenty of water and bring to the boil. Turn off the heat and leave for 1 hour. Drain. Warm olive oil in a medium saucepan and cook onion until translucent. Add whole garlic cloves and cook a couple of minutes more. Add chickpeas and cover with stock. Add water if the chickpeas are not well covered. Bring to the boil and simmer for $1^1/2$ hours, adding water occasionally as the liquid evaporates. The chickpeas are delicious served like this but are even better pureed in the food processor with salt and pepper to taste. Add extra water or olive oil for a runnier consistency.

Using cooked canned chickpeas: Heat olive oil in a small pan over medium heat. Cook onion for 2 minutes, add whole garlic cloves and cook 3 minutes more. Taste the liquid in the can of chickpeas – sometimes it has food acid in it which is not very palatable. If so, drain and rinse. Puree onion mixture in the food processor with chickpeas, including either 2 tablespoons of water or liquid from the can. Add salt, pepper and olive oil to taste. Return to pan over gentle heat.

Preheat char-grill or barbecue to hot. Cook whole lamb racks, turning frequently, for 15–20 minutes. Turn off grill and rest lamb in a warm place for 10 minutes. Serve whole or sliced into cutlets, with chickpea puree and steamed English spinach.

Choose almost any red wine to serve with this full-flavoured dish. If you prefer a white wine, try a chardonnay.

There's something very attractive about baby vegetables.
Here they are used to great effect with mini roasts,
available from your butcher.

lamb mini roasts
with baby beetroot and fennel

Serves 6

Preheat oven to moderately hot, 200°–210°C (400°–425°F) Gas Mark 5. Slice fennel and beetroot in half and place in a baking dish; brush with oil and bake for 10 minutes. Add lamb to dish and cook for 20 minutes only. Remove lamb and rest in a warm place for 10 minutes.

Keep fennel and beetroot hot in the oven. Deglaze the baking dish with stock, wine and redcurrant jelly and boil until reduced and thickened to a sauce.

Slice lamb and serve on individual plates with beetroot, fennel and sauce.

Choose a rounded, full-flavoured red wine, such as merlot, cabernet sauvignon, or a shiraz blend.

INGREDIENTS

3 baby fennel

1–2 bunches baby beetroot

olive oil

3 lamb rumps or round roasts

1$^1/_2$ cups (375ml/12fl oz) beef stock

$^3/_4$ cup (190ml/6fl oz) red wine

2 generous tablespoons redcurrant jelly

A complete meal in one pot is somehow very satisfying. And best of all there's so much less to wash up.

One-pot Wonders

pumpkin and coconut soup

Pumpkin soup is a perennial favourite in Australia. Here it is given an Asian twist with the addition of spice and coconut. Orange sweet potato can be substituted for the pumpkin, but it gives a thicker puree so you will need to add a little more stock.

INGREDIENTS

1 small or $1/2$ large butternut pumpkin, just over 1kg (2lbs) unpeeled

1 tablespoon olive oil

1 onion, chopped

1 teaspoon or more freshly grated ginger

1 teaspoon coriander (cilantro) seeds

$1^1/_2$ cups (375ml/12fl oz) chicken or vegetable stock

$1^1/_2$ cups (375ml/12fl oz) coconut milk

salt and freshly ground pepper

2 teaspoons lemon juice

$1/2$ bunch fresh coriander

Serves 4 as a main or 6 as an entree

Peel and seed pumpkin and cut into chunks. Heat a frying pan with some olive oil and cook onion, without browning, until softened. Increase heat and add ginger and coriander seeds. Add pumpkin, turning to coat in oil (about 1 minute). Add stock, cover pan and simmer for 10 minutes, or until pumpkin is soft. Puree contents of pan in a food processor, gradually adding coconut milk. Season to taste with salt, pepper and lemon juice.

To serve, ladle into bowls and sprinkle with fresh coriander leaves.

Serve with chilled sherry, or try a blended white wine, such as a semillon/chardonnay, semillon/sauvignon blanc or classic dry white three-blend style.

In a Malaysian night street market I was fascinated to see this dish prepared in a huge flat-bottomed wok over a gas burner. First the cook fried what looked like sambal oelek in oil with fish sauce. Then in went noodles, Asian greens and egg. Individual portions were topped with fresh chilli. The first time I made it (very successfully), I used 2 tablespoons Sakims Singapore Chilli, Lime & Cracked Pepper paste and 1 tablespoon Sakims Vietnamese Ginger & Shallot Paste, but here I have worked out an alternative paste.

fried rice noodles

INGREDIENTS

Serves 4 as a light meal or 6 as an accompaniment

Make a paste by grinding sambal oelek with ginger, eschalots and garlic. Fry in oil in a large pan over high heat. Add fish sauce and, when well combined, add drained, separated rice noodles and stir well to coat with the sauce. Add Asian greens, first the stems and a moment or two later the leaves. Add shallots and bean sprouts. When well combined and hot, move noodles to outside of pan, leaving some of the base clear in the centre. Add a little more oil and the beaten egg. Allow egg to set and shred it through the noodles. Taste noodles and if they need a bit more punch, stir through lime juice and kecap manis. Garnish with chilli, if desired.

Note: Buy fresh rice noodles in Asian shops and just run hot water over them, or else rehydrate the dried rice sticks in boiling water for 5–10 minutes.

Choose a fresh young white wine, such as a semillon or sauvignon blanc or a blend of the two, a riesling, or a light style of red wine, such as a rosé.

2 teaspoons sambal oelek or chilli paste

1 tablespoon fresh ginger, grated

2 large eschalots

2 cloves garlic

1–2 tablespoons peanut oil

1 tablespoon Thai fish sauce.

125g (4oz) dried or 250g (8oz) fresh rice noodles (see Note)

Asian greens e.g. choy sum, bok choy or gai laan, sliced

1/2 bunch green shallots, chopped

1 cup (80–100g/3–4oz) bean sprouts

1 egg, lightly beaten

juice of 1/2 lime or lemon

1–2 tablespoons kecap manis (sweet Indonesian soy sauce)

2 fresh chillies, sliced for garnish, optional

I invented this recipe when some very dear friends who are vegetarians came for dinner. It was a hit! I also served mushroom risotto and fresh asparagus.

slow-roasted vegetables

INGREDIENTS

2 bulbs of fennel, quartered (or cut into eighths if large)

extra virgin olive oil

8 pink fir apple potatoes or other waxy potatoes, halved

8 ripe tomatoes, halved

fresh rosemary sprigs

sea salt and freshly ground black pepper, to taste

Serves 6–8 as an accompaniment

Place fennel in an oven dish, splash liberally with olive oil and bake in a slow oven, 150°C (300°F) Gas Mark 2. After 30 minutes, add potatoes; after another 30 minutes, add tomatoes. Cook for 20–30 minutes longer. Remove vegetables from oven. Place in a large warm bowl and toss with a little olive oil, rosemary sprigs, salt and pepper.

Choose any full-flavoured wine, from chardonnay to cabernet, to serve with these delicious vegetables.

cataplana

Shellfish and pork is a popular combination in Portugal. Legend has it that it was used during the Inquisition as a double whammy to test religious zeal as pork and shellfish are forbidden to Jews and Moslems.

Serves 6

To clean clams, soak in plenty of cold water with salt and cornmeal added for at least 30 minutes. This purges the clams of grit. Rinse, wash, and rinse again.

Heat oil and cook onion over low heat until it begins to soften. Add capsicum and garlic and cook until all are softened, sweet and soft but not brown. Increase heat and add bay leaf, tomato, tomato paste and wine and bring to the boil. Reduce heat to medium and simmer until tomato is broken down and the sauce is pulpy. Stir in prosciutto or ham and chourico and cook for 5 minutes more.

Add clams to pot, mix through the sauce and cover with a tight-fitting lid. Cook for only 3–5 minutes, or until clams open. (Discard any that do not open.) Serve immediately, sprinkled with parsley and seasoned with black pepper to taste.

Note: A cataplana is a hinged metal container that can be clamped shut. A pan with a tight-fitting lid works fine.

For this dish choose a rose or light style of red wine, such as pinot noir or chambourcin. For a different approach, try a chilled fino sherry.

INGREDIENTS

1 kg (2lbs) clams or vongole

$1/4$ cup salt, approx.

$1/4$ cup (40g/1oz) cornmeal (polenta), approx.

olive oil

1 medium Spanish onion, chopped

1 medium onion, chopped

1 red capsicum (red pepper)

3 cloves garlic, chopped

1 bay leaf

4 large red, ripe tomatoes, peeled, seeded and chopped

1 tablespoon tomato paste

$1/2$ cup (125ml/4fl oz) white wine

155g (5oz) piece prosciutto (presunto is the Portuguese style) or smoked ham

1 chourico (the Portuguese version), chorizo or pepperoni, coarsely chopped

2 tablespoons Continental parsley, chopped

freshly ground black pepper

Bastilla (or bisteeya) is the jewel of festive Moroccan cooking. In the traditional recipe the filling is spiced pigeon or chicken and almonds in ouarka pastry. This version is far easier.

seafood bastilla

INGREDIENTS

6 sheets filo pastry

8 tablespoons olive oil

cinnamon, to garnish

filling

1 small onion, diced

3 tablespoons olive oil

1 teaspoon sweet paprika

1 teaspoon ground cumin

1 teaspoon ground coriander (cilantro)

1 teaspoon turmeric

salt and freshly ground pepper

lemon juice

500g (1lb) mixed fillets firm, mild-flavoured fish e.g. salmon, ling

225g (8oz) shelled prawns

225g (8oz) squid or calamari, cut into strips

1/2 bunch parsley, chopped

1/2 bunch coriander, chopped

Serves 6

Preheat oven to moderately hot, 200°–210°C (400°–425°F) Gas Mark 5. For filling, cook onion in oil until softened. Add spices and cook 2 minutes more. Season to taste and sprinkle with a little lemon juice. Cool.

Meanwhile, chop seafood coarsely. Add parsley, coriander and cooled onion spice mixture. Brush a springform cake tin, about 23cm (9in), with oil and line with baking paper. Fold one sheet of filo in half and place in tin. Brush with oil. Repeat twice (i.e. 3 double layers in all), placing each fold of filo at a slight angle from the one underneath so that the sides of the tin are well covered. Fill with seafood mixture. Place a folded-over piece of filo on a flat oiled board. Brush with oil. Repeat twice (again, 3 double layers in all).

Quickly and carefully place filo and board upside-down over the tin filled with filo and seafood. Holding them carefully together, invert the tin and board so that the board is again on the bottom. Remove the side of the springform pan and fold ends of filo on the board up around the bastilla. Replace springform side and invert the whole tin and board again so that the filo-encased bastilla is all back in the tin. Make sure the top is well basted with oil. (At this point the bastilla can be wrapped in foil and frozen if you wish to prepare it ahead of time.) Bake for 15–20 minutes, or until golden brown. Serve immediately, cut into large wedges or the bastilla will become soggy.

It is traditional to decorate the bastilla with swirls of cinnamon and powdered sugar. However, a seafood bastilla is not traditional and the Australian palate does not usually like so much sweetness in a main course. The cinnamon makes a contribution though. Alternatively, put some cinnamon in the spice mix.

Choose a fragrant wine, such as a sauvignon blanc, riesling, dry gewurztraminer or soft red, to accompany this dish, which is more fragrant than spicy.

Many nations have a version of this dish. In Portugal,
it would customarily be served at the beginning of the
meal as one of a number of dishes placed on the table.

marinated baby octopus

Serves 6

If octopus are not already prepared, cut off their heads and remove and discard the small hard 'beak' that remains in the top.

Cover remaining tentacles with vinegar, onion, bay leaf and peppercorns and add cold water to cover, about 2 cups (500ml/18fl oz), depending on the size of the saucepan. Bring to the boil and drain immediately. Combine Spanish onion, chilli, garlic, lemon juice, olive oil and herbs and season to taste. Refrigerate until ready to serve. Serve with octopus and crusty bread.

Choose a rosé or light style of red wine.

INGREDIENTS

750g ($1\frac{1}{2}$ lbs) baby octopus

$\frac{1}{2}$ cup (125ml/4fl oz) red wine vinegar

$\frac{1}{2}$ onion, sliced

1 bay leaf

$\frac{1}{2}$ teaspoon whole black peppercorns

$\frac{1}{2}$ large Spanish onion, finely chopped

2 red chillies, finely chopped

2 cloves garlic, finely chopped

$\frac{1}{4}$ cup (60ml/2fl oz) lemon juice (1 small lemon)

1 cup (250ml/8fl oz) extra virgin olive oil

1 cup freshly chopped herbs, e.g. parsley, coriander (cilantro)

2 tablespoons freshly chopped mint

seafood paella

INGREDIENTS

2/3 cup (160ml/5fl oz) extra virgin olive oil

2 cloves garlic

1 teaspoon La Chinata hot or sweet smoked paprika

2 ripe tomatoes

500g (1lb) Calasparra rice (or short-grain rice)

500g (1lb) peeled green prawns

250g (8oz) calamari or cuttlefish, sliced

6 cups (1.5 litres/2 3/4 pints) prawn stock (see method)

pinch saffron threads, optional

salt

freshly chopped parsley, for garnish

stock

1/4 cup (60ml/2fl oz) extra virgin olive oil

2 cloves garlic

1 teaspoon La Chinata hot or sweet smoked paprika

2 ripe tomatoes, diced

shells and heads from prawns (see above)

7 cups (1.75 litres/3 pints) fish stock

I love to adapt the classic dishes of other countries to make them as simple as possible without losing flavour. This is my version of seafood paella. La Chinata, a Spanish smoked paprika, gives a wonderful flavour.

Serves 4–6

To prepare stock, heat oil in a large saucepan and cook garlic, paprika and tomato over medium heat. When brown, add prawn shells and heads and cover with stock. Bring to the boil and simmer for at least 30 minutes and preferably 1 hour. Strain, discarding solids.

In a paella pan (or heavy-based frying-pan with even heat distribution), heat 2 tablespoons oil and cook garlic, paprika and tomato, stirring frequently, until brown and pulpy. (This mixture, called picada or sofrito, is used in most seafood paellas in Spain.) Add remaining oil and rice, mix well and let rice brown for 2 minutes. Moisten with hot stock, mix well and bring to the boil over high heat for 5 minutes. Add seafood, saffron and salt to taste.

Reduce heat and let paella cook, without stirring, for 12–14 minutes longer. If you have a pan with very even heat distribution all cooking can be done on the cooktop. Otherwise, when the rice rises to the top, put the pan in a moderate oven, 180°–190°C (350°–375°F) Gas Mark 4, for 4 minutes. Cooking time should not exceed 19 minutes in all. Remove from oven, add parsley and leave to rest for at least 3 minutes before serving.

Choose a Spanish wine to accompany this Iberian classic, or a semillon, pinot noir or chambourcin.

I have been lucky enough to visit Portugal and enjoy the country's unique cuisine which, naturally enough in a seafaring nation, features lots of seafood. I found this delicious dish easy to reproduce here with clams, which are not used as often as they deserve to be.

Portuguese-style clams

Serves 4

To clean clams, soak in plenty of cold water with salt and cornmeal added for at least 30 minutes. This purges the clams of grit. Rinse, wash, and rinse again.

Heat olive oil in a frying-pan, add clams, wine, garlic and parsley. Cover and place over medium to high heat for a few minutes only – you will hear a cracking sound as the clams open. Once open, they are ready to eat. Serve immediately with fresh bread to sop up the juices.

Choose any light style of white wine, or even a rosé, with this dish.

INGREDIENTS

1kg (2lbs) clams or vongole

$1/4$ cup salt, approx.

$1/4$ cup cornmeal, approx.

1–2 tablespoons extra virgin olive oil

$1/4$–$1/2$ cup (60–125ml/2–4fl oz) white wine

2 cloves garlic, chopped

3 tablespoons flat-leaf parsley, freshly chopped

to serve

fresh bread (such as the wonderful Portuguese broa)

INGREDIENTS

315g (10oz) dried
rice noodles

1/4 cup (60ml/2fl oz) peanut oil

2 eggs, lightly beaten

1 medium onion, sliced

3 cloves garlic, finely chopped

220g (7oz) lean pork
(e.g. pork fillet), sliced

2 tablespoons dried shrimp

90g (3oz) bean curd, diced

pinch of chilli flakes

1/4 cup (60ml/2fl oz) lime juice (1–2 limes)

1/4 cup (60ml/2fl oz) Thai fish sauce

2 tablespoons palm sugar (or brown sugar)

1–2 cups (80–160g/3–6oz) bean sprouts

50g (1.5oz) roasted,
unsalted peanuts, chopped

2 tablespoons garlic chives, chopped

2 tablespoons coriander
(cilantro) leaves, chopped

to serve

lime wedges, optional

chilli flakes

This is one of the classics of Thai cuisine. Rice noodles are my favourite and I love this combination. Dried shrimp, used as a flavouring ingredient, are available at Asian supermarkets. Fresh prawns or chicken can be substituted for pork.

pad thai

Serves 4–6

Soak rice noodles in hot water for about 10 minutes, or until soft; drain. Heat 1 tablespoon oil in wok over medium heat and scramble the eggs. Remove and set aside. Heat remaining oil and fry onion for 1 minute before adding garlic. Continue to stir-fry until just beginning to brown. Increase heat to high, add pork and cook until pork is cooked through. Add shrimp, bean curd and chilli flakes. Stir through carefully and reduce heat to medium.

Add lime juice, fish sauce and sugar, stirring to dissolve. Add drained noodles and mix through. Add eggs and most of the bean sprouts, peanuts, chives and coriander. Toss all together. Serve immediately, garnished with remaining bean sprouts, peanuts, chives and coriander. Serve with lime wedges and a pile of chilli flakes.

Choose a white wine with some citrus character with this dish – perhaps a riesling, or unoaked chardonnay, or a young semillon.

INGREDIENTS

4 pieces chicken Maryland,
  preferably corn-fed free-range chicken

1 teaspoon ground cumin

1 teaspoon ground coriander (cilantro)

1 teaspoon ground cinnamon

salt and freshly ground black pepper

2 tablespoons olive oil

1 large onion, sliced

1 bulb of plump garlic,
  about 15 cloves, peeled

250g (8oz) button mushrooms

$1/2$ cup (125ml/4fl oz)
white wine

1 cup (250ml/8fl oz)
chicken stock

2 carrots, coarsely chopped

2 whole red chillies, cut in half
  but held together by the stem

1 knob fresh ginger,
  peeled and sliced

1 preserved lemon, skin only,
  cut into strips

1 cup (250ml/8fl oz) stock, extra

125g (4oz) couscous

This is a recipe I originally developed for a 'one-pot' story in **Australian Gourmet Traveller**. It was inspired by a trip to Morocco – but this is, once more, my version.

Serves 4

Preheat oven to moderate, 180°–190°C (350°–375°F) Gas Mark 4.

Rub chicken skin with combined cumin, coriander, cinnamon, salt and pepper. Warm 1 tablespoon oil in a large flameproof casserole and cook onion and garlic until lightly coloured. Add remaining oil and mushrooms and toss to coat with oil. Cook 2 minutes longer. Add wine and stock and bring to the boil. Add carrot, chillies, ginger and preserved lemon. Return to the boil. Plunge the chicken into this, turning it to tighten the skin. Seal casserole well with foil and a lid and bake, for 40 minutes. Alternatively, cook over very low heat on the cooktop.

Pour extra stock over couscous and leave to swell while the chicken is cooking. At the end of cooking time, remove chicken and add couscous to warm through in the wonderful broth and vegetables left in the pot. Replace chicken on top and stand, covered, for about 5 minutes.

To serve, ladle the aromatic broth with vegetables and couscous into 4 bowls and top each with a joint of chicken. Remove the chillies if you wish, but the long cooking will have transferred their flavour throughout the pot. The occasional bit of preserved lemon is a wonderful surprise.

Choose a young, unwooded semillon for a miraculous match with the preserved lemon in this dish.

chicken in a pot with preserved lemon

standing rib roast on vegetables

There's something very grand about standing ribs of beef. Sure, it takes a little longer to cook, but my version largely cooks itself in one roasting pan.

INGREDIENTS   Serves 6–8

1 medium eggplant (aubergine)

salt

1 standing rib roast, about 3 ribs

2 tablespoons sumac (see Note)

1 small head celeriac or 1/2 large one

2 tablespoons olive oil

2 onions, coarsely chopped

4 cloves garlic, smashed, optional

1 red capsicum (red pepper), cut into wide strips

salt and freshly ground black pepper

800g (1 1/2 lb) can diced tomatoes

3/4 cup (190ml/6fl oz) red wine

6 whole tomatoes, optional

Preheat oven to hot, 220°–230°C (450°–475°F) Gas Mark 6. Cut eggplant, lengthwise, into very large batons. Salt and leave to drain in a colander for 30 minutes. Rub roast with sumac, reserving remainder. Peel celeriac and cut into thin wedges. Keep in acidulated water to prevent browning. Rinse eggplant under running water and dry on paper towels, removing all excess moisture.

Heat baking dish and olive oil on cooktop. Add onion and celeriac and toss to coat with oil. Add eggplant after a few minutes. Cook over high heat, turning frequently. Add garlic and capsicum and cook a little longer. Sprinkle salt, pepper and remaining sumac over vegetable mixture, place roast on top and place in oven for 10 minutes. Remove from oven. Lift roast and pour canned tomatoes and wine over vegetables. Cover loosely with foil and place roast back on top of foil. Reduce heat to 200°–210°C (400°–425°F) Gas Mark 5 and return dish to oven. Cook for a further 25–30 minutes for medium rare.

Remove beef to a warm place to rest for at least 15 minutes. Remove foil and pour any juices that have collected on the foil into a saucepan. Add juices from vegetables, including the chopped tomato, which will have broken down to become saucy. Bring to the boil. Return vegetables plus fresh tomatoes to the hot oven while beef is resting. Stir sauce frequently — if you prefer a smoother texture puree it.

Place roast on a large platter surrounded by vegetables and pass sauce separately. Serve with baked potatoes and sugarsnap (mange tout) peas, if desired.

Note: Sumac is a berry-like fruit dried and ground to a purple powder. It is available from Lebanese delis or stockists of Middle Eastern spices.

Choose any robust or full-bodied red wine; cabernet sauvignon and blends, shiraz or durif would be admirable.

Grand or simple finales all have one thing in common — that wonderful sweet sensation left on the tongue …

Sweet Sensations

INGREDIENTS

6 ripe tomatoes, 90–125g (3–4oz) each

juice of 1/2 lemon

filling

1/2 mango, about 90g (3oz), very finely diced

1 pear, about 90g (3oz), very finely diced

10 mint leaves, chopped

1 teaspoon orange rind, finely chopped

2 teaspoons sugar

1 teaspoon ginger, chopped

syrup

1 1/4 cups (300ml/1/2 pint) freshly squeezed orange juice

2 vanilla pods, scraped out

3 cloves

rind of 2 oranges

315g (10oz) sugar

3 star anise

rind of 2 lemons

1/3 teaspoon curry powder

to serve

vanilla ice-cream

When Alain Verzeroli, French-trained Executive Chef at Restaurant Petrus at Island Shangri-La Hotel, gave a Masterclass in Melbourne in March 1998, he cooked an astonishing but complicated Confit of tomato stuffed with dried and fresh fruit flavoured with star anise and vanilla, served with an orange syrup. This is my humble and greatly simplified version – still delicious!

Serves 6

Make the syrup first, by placing all ingredients in a small saucepan and boiling for 5 minutes. Set aside.

To skin tomatoes, cut a cross in the bottom and immerse in boiling water for 30 seconds. Plunge into cold water. The skin will now peel off easily. Cut a slice from the stalk end and remove the seeds through the hole. Combine filling ingredients and stuff the tomatoes with it.

Place tomatoes in a saucepan with syrup and cook for 10 minutes, basting frequently with the syrup. (Alternatively, cook in a moderate oven, 180°–190°C (350°–375°F) Gas Mark 4, for about 15 minutes.) When tomatoes are candied, drizzle with lemon juice and cook for 1 minute longer. Serve warm or cold, topped with orange rind (from the syrup) and ice-cream.

Choose a luscious dessert wine to serve with fruit desserts.

confit tomato dessert

There is an absolutely glorious Middle Eastern cake made by boiling cleaned oranges for an hour, cooling them and then combining with almonds and separated eggs. I love it, but it is time-consuming to make and creates lots of washing up. This one is much simpler.

orange syrup cake

Serves 12

Preheat oven to moderately slow, 160°C (325°F) Gas Mark 3. Grease a 23cm (9in) cake tin (or larger) with extra light olive oil spray.

In a large microwave-safe mixing bowl heat butter, rind and caster sugar in microwave on high for 2 minutes. Beat with electric mixer and add eggs. Add buttermilk and flour in 2 batches, mixing only until just combined. Pour mixture into prepared tin and bake for 55–60 minutes.

Meanwhile, boil the orange juice and rind vigorously with the sugar until reduced to a thick syrup of coating consistency. Remove cake from oven and pour two-thirds of the syrup over the hot cake. Serve with remaining syrup and thick cream.

Choose a light, floral style of dessert wine with overtones of orange, or serve with orange liqueur, such as Grand Marnier, Cointreau of orange Curaçao.

INGREDIENTS

250g (8oz) butter

grated rind of 2 oranges

2 cups (440g/14oz) caster sugar

6 eggs

$1^1/_2$ cups (375ml/12fl oz) buttermilk

2 cups (300g/$9^1/_2$oz) self-raising flour

syrup

juice of 3 oranges

rind of 1 orange

60g (2oz) sugar

to serve

thick cream

Literally, **panna cotta** means cooked cream, but that doesn't really do justice to this smooth, silky Italian dessert. There are many different versions and buttermilk can be used instead of milk and/or cream for a lighter finish. While it is traditionally made on the cooktop, it's much quicker in the microwave.

panna cotta with strawberries

INGREDIENTS

Serves 4

4 leaves of gelatine
(or 2 teaspoons gelatine powder)

1$^1/_4$ cups (300ml/$^1/_2$ pint) cream

$^3/_4$ cup (190ml/6fl oz) milk

1 tablespoon caster sugar

1 teaspoon vanilla extract
or orange flower water or liqueur

to serve

250g (8oz) fresh strawberries

1 teaspoon sugar

splash of liqueur e.g. Grand Marnier,
Cointreau (optional)

extra fresh strawberries,
to decorate (optional)

Soften gelatine by soaking in cold water. Meanwhile, heat cream, milk and caster sugar in the microwave until just under boiling point. Stir to dissolve sugar. Squeeze gelatine sheets to remove excess water and stir into hot cream mixture with vanilla extract until gelatine is completely melted. (If you use gelatine powder, strain the mixture.) Stir occasionally as mixture cools.

Lightly grease 4 ramekins or dariole moulds with light olive oil spray (or rinse with cold water) and pour in mixture. Cool and chill for at least 5–6 hours. To turn out, run a knife around the edges and/or dip ramekins very briefly in hot water. Invert onto plates and serve with fresh strawberries pureed with a touch of sugar and liqueur. Decorate with extra strawberries, if desired.

Choose any light style of dessert wine to serve with this light and delicate dessert.

I love a good tarte tatin, especially made with pear or quince, but who has time to make one? This simple method is devastatingly delicious!

rhubarb tarte tatin

Serves 6

Preheat oven to hot, 220°–230°C (450°–475°F) Gas Mark 6. Make a caramel by heating sugar and water over high heat until medium caramel colour (about 10 minutes). Stir before it comes to the boil to dissolve the sugar, but not after it has come to the boil. Remove from heat and immediately thin with Grand Marnier. (Take care as it may splutter!)

Pour into greased ovenproof pan or dish – I use an oval 22cm x 36cm (9in x 14in) but a slab pan, 20cm x 30cm (8in x 12in), works well, too. Add rhubarb and sprinkle with extra sugar. Cut the puff pastry sheet to fit the pan and place on the rhubarb. Cook in oven for 12–15 minutes or until pastry is golden.

Remove from oven and rest for 5 minutes. Drain any excess juice released by the rhubarb into a jug and pass separately as sauce. Carefully place a board over the entire dish and invert quickly. Cut into slices and serve with thick cream and reserved rhubarb juice.

Choose a fresh, fruity style of dessert wine, such as a late-picked riesling.

INGREDIENTS

1 cup (220g/7oz) sugar

$1/3$ cup (80ml/$2^1/2$fl oz) water

$1/4$ cup (60ml/2fl oz) Grand Marnier or Cointreau

1 bunch rhubarb, cut into 10cm (4in) lengths

1 tablespoon sugar, extra

1 or 2 sheets butter puff pastry

thick cream, to serve

Chocolate and raspberries are universally popular.
Put them together and you have a real winner
in this deluxe version of a self-saucing pudding.

chocolate raspberry puddings

INGREDIENTS

2 tablespoons butter

$^1/_3$ cup (50g/2oz) loosely packed brown sugar

1 egg

$^3/_4$ cup (110g/3$^1/_2$oz) self-raising flour

1 tablespoon Dutch (or other good-quality) cocoa

$^1/_3$ cup (80ml/2$^1/_2$fl oz) milk

2 punnets raspberries

$^1/_3$ cup coarsely grated chocolate

sauce

$^1/_4$ cup (40g/1$^1/_2$oz) loosely packed brown sugar

2 teaspoons Dutch (or other good-quality) cocoa

$^3/_4$ cup (190ml/6fl oz) boiling water

to serve

thick cream

Serves 4

Preheat oven to moderate, 180°–190°C (350°–375°F) Gas Mark 4. Spray 4 x $^1/_2$-cup (125ml) ramekins with extra light olive oil spray (or grease with butter). Place on a flat baking tray.

Beat butter and sugar together until pale. Add egg and beat again until combined. Add flour, cocoa and milk and stir just until combined. Spoon half into the greased ramekins. Put 5 or 6 raspberries in each and sprinkle over 1 tablespoon chocolate. Top with remaining pudding mixture.

For sauce, mix together sugar and cocoa and sprinkle evenly over each pudding. Pour boiling water gently over the puddings (about 2 tablespoons on each). Bake for about 20 minutes. A skewer inserted in the top may not come out clean because of the sauce that forms underneath so be careful not to overcook. Serve with remaining raspberries and thick cream.

Choose a fortified style such as muscat, tokay or even port – chocolate has such an intensity of flavour that it can flatten out dessert wines that don't have the sugar level to stand up to it.

142

lemon polenta cake with lemon mascarpone

Polenta cakes have a long tradition in Italy. This recipe comes from my friend Luci Lothringer, who adapted it from one her mother used to make.

Serves 12–16

You will need five or six juicy lemons for this recipe, and two more if you decorate with shreds of rind as suggested.

Preheat oven to moderately slow, 160°C (325°F) Gas Mark 3. Grease a 26cm (10in) springform cake tin with extra light olive oil spray and line base with baking paper.

Cream butter and sugar until pale, then slowly beat in eggs, one at a time. Stir in vanilla, lemon rind and juice, then fold in almond meal, polenta, baking powder and salt. Pour into cake tin and bake for 30 minutes. Cover with foil and bake for 1 hour more, or until a skewer inserted into the centre comes out clean. Remove from oven, cool. Serve with lemon mascarpone.

To make lemon mascarpone, combine all ingredients in a food processor, taking care not to overbeat.

Note: Glazed lemon rind makes an attractive decoration for this cake. Bring 1/2 cup (125ml/4fl oz) water to the boil with 1/2 cup (110g/4oz) sugar, add the shredded rind of 2 lemons and simmer for 10 minutes, or until rind softens and is glazed with sugar.

Choose a late-picked or botrytised riesling to serve with this delicious cake.

INGREDIENTS

500g (1lb) unsalted butter, softened

500g (1lb) caster sugar

6 eggs

1/2 teaspoon vanilla essence

rind of 4 lemons

3/4 cup (190ml/6fl oz) lemon juice (3 lemons)

410g (13oz) almond meal

280g (9oz) polenta (cornmeal)

1 1/2 teaspoon baking powder

pinch salt

lemon mascarpone

2 tablespoons brandy

1 cup (220g/7oz) caster sugar

rind of 1 lemon

1/4 cup (60ml/2fl oz) lemon juice

3/4 cup (190ml/6fl oz) milk, or 1/3 cup (80ml/2 1/2fl oz) dry white wine

500g (1lb) mascarpone

I love the lime oil that's now available. I used it to great effect with prawns and snow peas in my book **Flavours**, and it occurred to me that it would be delicious to use just a touch in a dessert. This one is wondrously light and features one of my favourite combinations, red papaya and lime. If you can't get hold of lime oil, use some lime juice and lots of lime rind.

lime panna cotta

INGREDIENTS

Serves 8

4 or 5 leaves of gelatine
(or 2 teaspoons gelatine powder)

1 cup (250ml/8fl oz) cream

3 cups (750ml/24fl oz) milk

90g (3oz) sugar

1 teaspoon lime oil

extra light olive oil spray

to serve

1 lime, finely sliced

1 small red papaya,
peeled and finely sliced

Soak gelatine leaves in cold water. Bring cream and milk to the boil, either in a saucepan or in the microwave, adding sugar and stirring to dissolve once mixture is warm. Stir through lime oil and drained, squeezed-out gelatine leaves. (If you use gelatine powder, strain the mixture.) Leave to cool, stirring occasionally. (If you don't do this while the mixture cools, it will separate when set, the cream component sinking to the bottom. It still looks fine, though, and tastes delicious.)

Spray 8 dariole moulds with olive oil (or rinse with cold water) and pour in mixture. Leave to set overnight. To turn out, run a knife around the edges and/or dip moulds very briefly in hot water. Invert onto plates and serve — they should shimmy and shake! Serve with lime and papaya slices.

Choose a champagne or sparkling wine with some residual sugar, a sparkling rosé, or a lighter style of dessert wine such as a late-picked riesling — something not too sweet and cloying.

caramelised apple cake

The use of spices in this cake is optional. If you prefer your cake plain, leave them out. The addition of caramel makes a delicious, gooey cake.

Serves 8

Preheat oven to moderately slow, 160°C (325°F) Gas Mark 3. Grease a 23cm (9in) springform cake tin.

Cream butter, sugar and lemon rind until light and fluffy. Add eggs, one at a time, combining thoroughly after each addition. Beat in the flours and spices (if using), add cream and milk and beat again to a smooth batter. Spread half the mixture over base of prepared tin.

Meanwhile, peel, quarter and core apples and slice thinly. Layer half over the cake mixture. Drizzle with half the caramel sauce. Top with remaining cake mixture and apples. Bake for about 45 minutes. Drizzle with remaining caramel sauce and return to the oven for 10–15 minutes, or until cooked. Stand in the pan for 5 minutes, then remove the springform sides and cool on the base.

Serve warm with cream or ice-cream.

This cake is sticky and lush and it is best served with good strong coffee.

INGREDIENTS

125g (4oz) butter

^{2}/$_3$ cup (155g/5oz) caster sugar

1 teaspoon grated lemon rind

2 eggs

1 cup (155g/5oz) self-raising flour

^{1}/$_2$ cup (75g) plain flour

^{1}/$_2$ teaspoon ground nutmeg

^{1}/$_2$ teaspoon ground cinnamon

^{1}/$_2$ teaspoon ground ginger

^{1}/$_2$ cup (125ml/4fl oz) thick sour cream

^{1}/$_4$ cup (60ml/2fl oz) milk

2 or 3 apples

^{1}/$_2$ cup (125ml/4fl oz) purchased caramel sauce

coeur à la crème

This is an oldie, but a goodie, a great dessert for lovers. You need perforated heart-shaped moulds as the creme must drain overnight. Lining the moulds with muslin gives an attractive texture to the hearts and also makes them easier to turn out. For a sharper flavour, use half yoghurt and half cream.

INGREDIENTS

250g (8oz) mascarpone

1¼ cups (300ml/½pint) thickened cream

1 tablespoon vanilla sugar

1 tablespoon Cognac, Grand Marnier or Cointreau

berry puree

1 punnet (250g/8oz) berries, e.g. strawberries or raspberries

1 tablespoon caster sugar or more, to taste

1 punnet (250g/8oz) berries, extra, for decoration

mint leaves

Serves 6 (or 8 with slightly smaller hearts)

Line heart-shaped moulds with wet muslin. Blend mascarpone with cream (or cream and yoghurt), sugar and liqueur, taking care not to overbeat. Fill prepared moulds, place on a tray and leave to drain in the refrigerator for several hours, preferably overnight.

Puree berries with sugar and spoon a little onto individual serving plates. Unmould hearts on top, removing the muslin once the hearts are in place, and decorate with extra berries and mint leaves.

Choose a rich, full-bodied dessert wine, such as a botrytised semillon or riesling.

These keep very well and are delicious served with coffee.

macadamia and espresso biscotti

Makes about 30

Preheat oven to moderate, 180°–190°C (350°–375°F) Gas Mark 4.
Chop coffee beans in a food processor. Add flour and baking powder and
mix. Add butter and pulse until mixture resembles fine breadcrumbs. Add
caster sugar and pulse again. Briefly mix in macadamia nuts. Remove from
processor to a bowl and mix in brewed espresso and eggs. (This can all be
done in the processor but take care not to overmix or chop macadamias too
finely.) Knead together into a ball. Divide dough in halves and roll into 2 logs
about 5cm (2ins) wide, flattening slightly on top.

Place well apart on a oven tray lined with baking paper and bake for 40–45
minutes, or until cooked through. Remove and allow to cool for 20 minutes.
Cut into 2.5cm (1in) thick slices and bake on an oven tray at moderate,
180°–190°C (350°–375°F) Gas Mark 4, for 8 minutes. Turn biscotti over and
bake for a further 8 minutes, or until golden brown. Cool and store in an
airtight container.

**Naturally enough, these go with coffee and perhaps a fortified
wine, such as port, tokay or muscat, at the end of a meal.**

INGREDIENTS

45g (1^1/$_2$oz) espresso
coffee beans

2^3/$_4$ cups (410g/13oz) plain flour

1^1/$_2$ teaspoons baking powder

60g (2oz) butter, diced

1 cup (220g/7oz) caster sugar

125g (4oz) toasted
macadamia nuts

1 tablespoon very strong,
freshly brewed espresso coffee

2 eggs

Forget everything you've heard about not making chocolates in summer. These are fine made then or at any time of year.

chocolate truffles

Makes 30 truffles

Bring cream to the boil and simmer until thick and bubbly and reduced by about half. Melt chocolate in the microwave, or over hot water in a double boiler, and stir into cream until smooth. Stir in liqueur to flavour. Cool, stirring occasionally, until thick enough to pipe. Using a piping bag, pipe chocolate mixture into rosettes in paper cases and dust with cocoa, if desired. Refrigerate before serving.

Note: Remember, better quality chocolate makes better truffles, but how much chocolate you use is up to you. More chocolate will make a firmer truffle; less will make a soft truffle that needs closer attention to refrigeration.

With chocolate, choose a liqueur muscat or tokay, a particular specialty of Rutherglen, but also made in other areas of Australia. Alternatively, serve with port or good coffee.

INGREDIENTS

1¼ cups (300ml/½ pint) cream

155–220g (5–7oz) dark couverture chocolate (not compound)

1–2 tablespoons liqueur, e.g. Cointreau, Grand Marnier

cocoa, for dusting (optional)

this goes with this...

Some combinations to get you going.

asian feast

Choose some, or all, depending on how many you are serving:
deep-fried bean curd with chilli sauce, fried rice noodles, spicy pork stir-fry
with noodles or barramundi achari, green pawpaw salad, glass noodle salad,
Asian-style roast pork salad, lime panna cotta

middle eastern feast

bessara, chicken, preserved lemon and green olive kofta,
seafood bastilla, lamb with tarator sauce, orange syrup cake

vegetarian feast

tapenade, pumpkin and coconut soup, slow-roasted vegetables,
wild mushroom pasta, confit tomato dessert

family sunday lunch

tomato tarts with fetta and tapenade, standing rib roast on vegetables,
chocolate raspberry puddings

mid-week dinner

prawns poached in lemon grass broth, spiced quail with nam jim,
confit tomato dessert

romantic dinner

scallops steamed with ginger, shallot and sesame, crisp-skinned
salmon with multi-coloured capsicum, coeur à la crème

lunch with friends

asparagus on garlicky bean puree with crisp pancetta, prawn
risotto with saffron, lemon polenta cake with lemon mascarpone

stylish dinner

polenta canapes with prawns, lamb mini roasts with beetroot
and fennel or veal with anchovy sauce, rhubarb tarte tatin,
chocolate truffles

festive dinner

scallops on the shell with Asian-style vinaigrette, spatchcock
dijonnaise, panna cotta with strawberries

portuguese flavours

marinated baby octopus, cataplana, oranges with honey and olive oil

tastebud teasers

king prawns with harissa sauce, thai-style red curry of chicken livers,
watermelon with iced gin

index